Hiking through History
New York

Exploring the Empire State's Past by Trail
from Youngstown to Montauk

Randi Minetor
Photos by Nic Minetor

FALCON GUIDES

GUILFORD, CONNECTICUT
HELENA, MONTANA

An imprint of Rowman & Littlefield
Falcon and FalconGuides are registered trademarks and Make Adventure Your Story is a trademark of Rowman & Littlefield.

Distributed by NATIONAL BOOK NETWORK

Copyright © 2016 Rowman & Littlefield
Maps by Deanta Global © Rowman & Littlefield
All photos by Nic Minetor

British Library Cataloguing-in-Publication Information Available

Library of Congress Cataloging-in-Publication Data Available
ISBN 978-1-4930-1953-3 (paperback)
ISBN 978-1-4930-1954-0 (e-book)

∞™ The paper used in this publication meets the minimum requirements of American National Standard for Information Sciences—Permanence of Paper for Printed Library Materials, ANSI/NISO Z39.48-1992.

The author and Rowman & Littlefield assume no liability for accidents happening to, or injuries sustained by, readers who engage in the activities described in this book.

Contents

The Hikes

CANADA
UNITED STATES

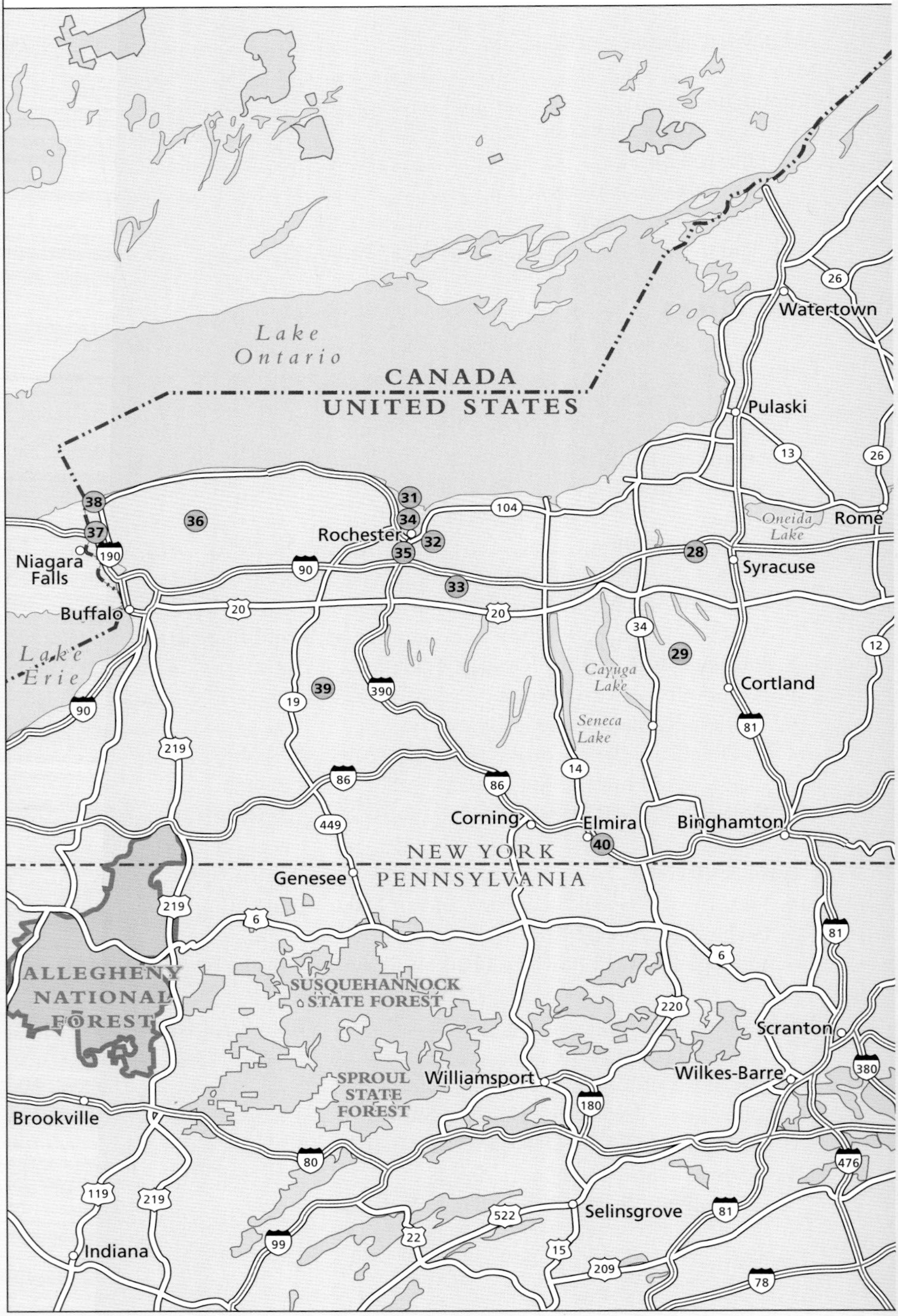

Lake Ontario

Watertown

Pulaski

Rome

Oneida Lake

Syracuse

26

13

26

104

31
34
32
35
33

Rochester

36

38
37
190

Niagara Falls

Buffalo

Lake Erie

90

20

90

20

28

34

29

Cortland

12

81

219

19

39

390

86

449

86

14

Corning

Elmira
40

Binghamton

NEW YORK
PENNSYLVANIA

Genesee

6

81

ALLEGHENY NATIONAL FOREST

SUSQUEHANNOCK STATE FOREST

220

6

Scranton

Wilkes-Barre

380

SPROUL STATE FOREST

Williamsport

180

Brookville

80

119
219

99

22

522

Selinsgrove

81

476

Indiana

15

209

78

Cayuga Lake

Seneca Lake

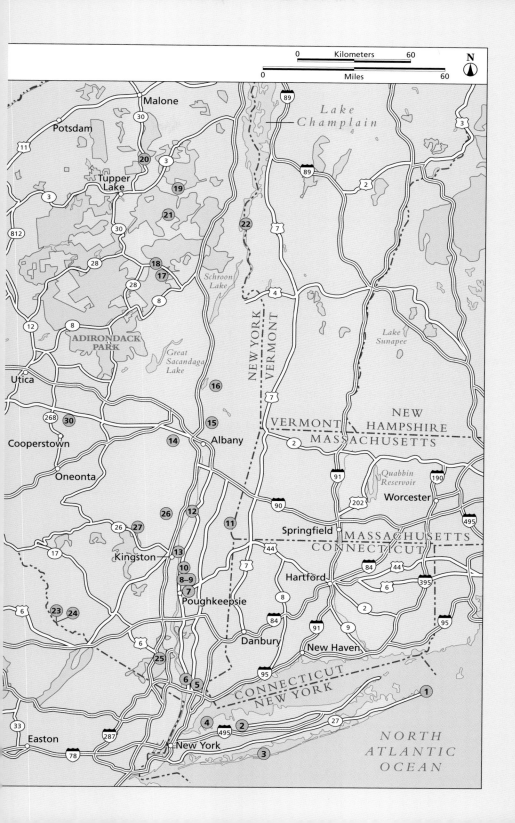

Acknowledgments

To all of the people who pointed us in various directions across the state to find things like the Tahawus ghost town, the Hooper garnet mine, the historic sites in Highland Park, and the battlefield at Newtown, we thank you for your willingness to share information—and to be part of our ongoing efforts to introduce hikers to some of the most interesting places in New York.

As always, many thanks to the team at FalconGuides for their fine work in bringing this project together, and to our agent, Regina Ryan, who does so much to keep our book writing/photographing careers on track.

And to the people who preserve these historic places—from the National Park Service to the neighborhood grassroots groups and volunteers—we thank you for keeping track of so much of our state's heritage. Without you, these fragments of times gone by would be housing developments, shopping malls, and parking lots instead of the fascinating places you have allowed us to discover.

Map Legend

Municipal

≡(84)≡ Interstate Highway

≡(20)≡ US Highway

≡(110)≡ State Road

≡[21]≡ Local/County Road

= = = = Unpaved Road

⊢—⊢—⊢ Railroad

— - - — - State Boundary

——— Leader line

|||||||||||||| Boardwalk

Trails

- - - - - - Featured Trail

- - - - - - Trail

——— Paved Trail/Bike path

Water Features

⬭ Body of Water

Marsh/Swamp

⌇ River/Creek

≋ Waterfall

Symbols

≍ Bridge

▪ Building/Point of Interest

∩ Cavern/Cave/Natural Bridge

† Cemetery

▬ Dam

⸸ Gate

🗼 Lighthouse

🅿 Parking

▲ Peak/Mountain

🎪 Picnic Area

🚻 Restroom

🔭 Scenic View/Lookout

🏛 Tower

○ Town

↗ Trail arrows

(20) Trailhead

❓ Visitor/Information Center

Land Management

🌲 National Park/Forest

🏔 State/County Park

░░░ Sand

Introduction

What a happy collision of two passions—one for American history, the other for New York's wide, wonderful outdoors—came together to create this book. *Hiking through History New York* is a book for people who like a little time travel with their walk in the woods, an opportunity to discover a piece of local history that you may never have happened across before. Here you will learn about the role of the Iroquois Confederacy in the Revolutionary War, the famous people buried on a Rochester hillside and their combined impact on the common people of America, the battles that changed the direction of wars as far back as the 1600s, the critical importance of New York's waterways to a growing nation, and the lives of the very rich and famous from Hyde Park to the heart of the Catskills.

So much of New York's development had a direct impact on the growth of America as a whole, so it's easy to feel the momentum of an entire country coursing forward in these historic places throughout our state. Ironworks turned ore from the Adirondack and Taconic Mountains into the raw materials industries needed, while men with pickaxes chipped garnets out of rock walls high in the North Country.

On the eastern end of Long Island, many trails lead to the Atlantic Ocean and pristine beach.

People with the vision to see connections over land propelled their ideas forward, building the Erie Canal and opening a water route to new territories to the west. Logging operations brought charcoal to ironworkers, wood to builders, and paper pulp to factories, while workers with "indoor jobs" turned out millions of shirt collars on an island where the Mohawk and Hudson Rivers meet.

At the same time, New York's history is filled with ordinary people growing up to do extraordinary things. In a corner of western New York, one woman became the first female ever to run for president of the United States, while another put her life at risk by walking into the polling place and casting her vote. An escaped slave became one of the nation's most respected orators and abolitionists, and a print shop worker invented a new style of poetry. Artists who saw the world differently from their Impressionist counterparts in Europe created the first truly American style of landscape painting. People of considerable means put their money to work for the greater good, and people of limited means tried—and sometimes failed—to change their lives for the better.

Such is the history of New York State, and your discovery of these stories and more begins with a single step.

Hikes in the Catskill Mountains reveal hidden lakes and expansive views.

How to Use This Guide

The hikes in this guide are listed by region, moving east to west across the state, making it simple for New York residents to reference the hikes just down the road or within an hour's drive, or to plan a day or weekend trip.

Whether your fondness for falling water impels you to scale granite walls to feel the spray or you prefer to take in a stunning view from the comfort of your van's front seat—or something in between—check out the Trail Finder that follows this introduction. We've supplied a listing of hikes that provide slices of military, Native American, industrial, and literary history, to help you find the locations and stories that appeal to you most.

We've assigned a difficulty rating for each hike, from "easy" to "very challenging." Choose hikes that match your experience and ability; there are plenty of fascinating places that do not require you to be in Schwarzenegger shape before you leave the house.

The description of each hike provides you with the detail you need up front, including length of the hike, fees, seasonal restrictions, the GPS coordinates for each trailhead or parking area, the length of the hike in distance and time, and where to call or navigate to for more information. Read through all of this before starting out, and follow the maps and step-by-step directions to reach your destination safely.

Hiking Tips

New York features many different kinds of terrain, from shale-covered glacial moraine to grassy slopes that become muddy and slippery with a little rain. And speaking of rain, New York has quite a bit of that, as well as more than 170 inches of snow each winter in some upstate areas. You'll want to be ready for the hazards that might lie ahead.

Wear appropriate footwear. Ankle support can make all the difference when you're hiking on rocky trails and rock-hopping across streams. There's nothing worse than having your hike or vacation spoiled by a sprained ankle you got when your foot unexpectedly slipped off a ledge—and I speak from experience. Wear hiking shoes that give you arch support and protect your toes, and opt for hiking boots with ankle support if you' re taking on an Adirondack or Catskill trail. Leave the flip-flops or slides at home.

Note: A properly fit pair of boots should feel comfortable from the first day you wear them—they should not need "breaking in." Buy your boots from an outfitter with knowledgeable sales staff to be sure you're getting the best advice.

Bring clothing for changeable weather—including a waterproof rain jacket or poncho—even on a sunny day. New York State weather can be changeable with little warning, especially in the high country. Storms can pop up in the mountains in minutes, turning a sunny morning into a soggy downpour. If you hike in winter, dress

The Hooper Garnet Mine is one of many silenced and reclaimed industrial sites in the Adirondacks.

in layers that you can remove during the uphill stretches and put back on to keep from getting chilled once you've cooled down.

Bring food and water. If you're going on a long day hike, bring at least one full meal and some salty/sweet snacks, like trail mix. Much of the hiking in this book involves uphill stretches, which can lengthen the time you're on the trail. You're going to need more water than you think, so plan on a pint per hour and bring at least an extra hour's worth. You may be tempted to refill your water bottles on the trail from a stream, but waterways often carry waterborne bacteria and protozoa that can cause serious illnesses. If you want to depend on streams for your water supply, it's imperative that you carry some type of water filtration system.

Know where you're going. Bring this book with you, and find or download additional maps as indicated in each hike description. Learn to use a compass, and bring one along—or a GPS device if you're comfortable with that technology. Remember that your smartphone's GPS capability may not work if you don't have cell service. New York's most rural and most mountainous areas still are not on anyone's coverage map.

Protect against bugs. Bring insect repellent that shields you from deer ticks and mosquitoes. Deer ticks can carry Lyme disease and mosquitoes West Nile virus, and they thrive in New York's forested regions and grassy areas. Even a walk in the grass alongside a road can scare up a mess of deer ticks. If you're going to walk through a field with high vegetation that will brush against your legs, long pants are strongly recommended.

Wear sunscreen, even on a cloudy day. While most of the hikes in this book take you through forested areas, you will find yourself in bright sunlight on open roads and on any kind of summit, even the low ones. Snow is also a powerful sunlight reflector, so if you're hiking in winter, apply sunscreen to any exposed skin before you start out.

Tell someone. Let someone know where you're going and when you expect to be back. Always sign the trail registries (when they're available) at the beginning and end of your hike. Don't expect to rely on your mobile phone; as I noted above, wide areas of the Adirondacks and Catskills have no cellular service, let alone 3G, 4G, or wireless. Even the rural areas between the western New York State Thruway exits can be cellular-free.

Never hike alone. First, it's not nearly as much fun as hiking with a buddy. Second, see or read *127 Hours*. You just never know when you're going to turn your ankle—or get your arm caught in a crevice—and find yourself stuck miles from the nearest road.

Paul Smith's College does a superb job of removing invasive species and restoring natural landscapes.

Read the signs. Nature preserves and state parks post signs to alert you to potential hazards within their boundaries, and it's always better to know what to expect. New York State has its fair share of wilderness obstacles—watch out for poison ivy, ticks, mosquitoes, timber rattlesnakes—yes, that's a remote possibility—or black bears.

Stay on the trail. You will be safer from poison ivy and bugs if you stick to the beaten path, and the forests and fields you cross will be safer as well. Stepping off the path can damage fragile ecosystems often found near water, like native vegetation and wildflowers. Resist the urge to cut across switchbacks or take unmarked, unauthorized shortcuts.

Use a walking stick. Some walks can involve stepping into murky water with little to no idea what's on the bottom of the stream, as well as walking on slick slabs of rock that turn out to be less stable than they appear. We highly recommend the use of a walking stick for hikes like these. Having a third point of contact with the ground can help you maintain your balance, brace you against falls, and find your best footing when you can't see below the surface. A walking stick or a pair of ski poles can be invaluable for winter hiking and for treks on steep, rocky trails.

Don't miss the opportunity to see Highland Park's collection of 1,200 lilac bushes in full bloom every May.

The view from Olana State Historic Site has been painted by several artists of the famous Hudson River School.

Let's Talk about Bears

Bear safety has become a real thing in New York, and not just deep in the Adirondacks. Black bears have been spotted on the Erie Canalway Trail near Rochester, in suburbs and smaller towns in the southern tier, and all over the Catskills and the Hudson River Valley. Here's what you should do on trail to avoid any kind of trouble with bears:

- **Make noise when hiking.** Bears have only average hearing and rather poor eyesight. Make plenty of noise when you're hiking—talk, sing, call out, and clap your hands at regular intervals. Bear bells generally are not loud enough to let the animals know you're on your way. Once the bear hears you coming, chances are good that he or she will move away from the trail and leave you alone.

- **Assume the bears are nearby.** Even the most popular and well-used trails may go through bear country, so don't assume that there are no bears there because so many people hike there daily. Keep making noise (and ignore the people who give you the evil eye for being noisy), and keep your eyes open for bears in the area.

- **Watch out for surprises.** When you approach streams, shrubs full of berries, fields of cow parsnip, or areas of dense vegetation, keep your eyes open for bears. As they can't always smell or hear you, you may startle a bear by arriving fairly quietly.
- **Do not approach bears.** Bears are not tame, and they are not zoo animals. You have come to their natural habitat in the wild, so you want to steer clear of them as much as possible. Don't try to get closer for a better photo. While deaths from bear attacks have been scant throughout New York's history, hikers in other states and in national parks have been mauled and sustained serious injuries because they tried to get too close.
- **Carry bear spray.** Pepper spray is one good defense against a charging bear. Nontoxic and with no permanent effect, it triggers "temporary incapacitating discomfort" in the bear, which can halt an attack and give you the opportunity to get away from the bear. If a bear charges you, aim the aerosol directly in the bear's face. This is not a bear repellent—spraying it on yourself (as you would an insect repellent) will not keep bears away.

Visit the grave of abolitionist and orator Frederick Douglass in Rochester.

- **If you encounter a bear, do this.** As every bear will react differently to you, there is no set protocol that will result in a sure-fire escape.
  - Try to detour around the bear if possible.
  - Do not run! Back away slowly, but stop if it seems to agitate the bear.
  - Make noise, wave your arms, and stand your ground.
  - Use peripheral vision. Bears may interpret direct eye contact as threatening.
  - Drop something (not food) to distract the bear. Keep your pack on for protection in case of an attack.
  - If a bear attacks and you have pepper spray, use it!
  - If the bear does attack you, fight back with all of your strength. Play dead *only* if you are certain that the bear is a mother protecting her cubs.
- **Store food safely.** When bears find human food in campsites, they learn to come back to these campsites again and again to devour table scraps or plunder trash cans. These bears can lose their aversion to humans and begin to see us as prey.

Be Good to Nature

A love of natural spaces is a wonderful thing, but New York's most beautiful areas are in danger of being loved to death. You can help preserve fragile lands; protect endangered species of plants, insects, and animals; and keep wild places as wild as they should be by following a few simple guidelines.

Pack out what you pack in. If you picnic or stop off to rest and have a snack, check the area to be sure you've cleaned up your trash.

Think before you pee. When you've got to go, remember to choose a spot at least 200 feet from the nearest body of water. Resist the temptation to urinate right on the trail; this can attract salt-loving animals, which could prove hazardous for you. Carry a trash bag and pack out your toilet tissue. If you're leaving something behind, bury your waste.

Take pictures and memories. Follow the words of Chief Si'ahl, the Duwamish chief for whom the city of Seattle is named, in his famous speech of 1854: "Take nothing but memories, leave nothing but footprints." Today we take memories in the form of pictures, but the spirit is the same. Leave the wildflowers, leaves, pinecones, rocks, and caterpillars for others to enjoy as much as you did, and share the best of New York State with countless others who will tread these paths after you do.

Do not approach wildlife. Chances are you don't need to be told not to poke a rattlesnake with a stick, but you may be tempted to feed squirrels and chipmunks. Please don't do this. It's not good for the animals, because they become habituated to human food and will become more and more aggressive about obtaining it. Bears, porcupines, foxes, coyotes, deer, birds, and small furry critters should be enjoyed from a distance. This goes double for geese and ducks that you may encounter near ponds or in city parks—when humans feed these birds bread and corn, the birds gather close together to get it, and this spreads infectious diseases among them. Just don't do it.

Keep your dog on a leash. Only a handful of trail managers actually prohibit dogs, but no park or trail manager in this book permits dogs to run free. Dogs are quick to sniff out burrowing animals, nesting birds, and other critters, and while most dogs only want to play, the animals they discover have no frame of reference for this. When dogs encounter larger animals—especially in bear country—the confrontation won't be good for anyone. Keep your dog leashed and close to you, especially when there are other animals around. And for heaven's sake, pick up your dog's droppings and carry them out of the park.

Irises line many trails in New York during the spring bloom.

Trail Finder

Best Hikes for Military History	
1	Camp Hero State Park
16	Saratoga National Historical Park: Wilkinson National Recreation Trail
19	John Brown Farm State Historic Site
22	Crown Point State Historic Site to Vermont
24	Minisink Battleground
37	Devil's Hole State Park
38	Old Fort Niagara State Historic Site / Beach Trail
40	Newtown Battlefield State Park
Best Hikes for Native American History	
14	John Boyd Thacher State Park: Indian Ladder Trail
24	Minisink Battleground
33	Ganondagan State Historic Site: The Earth Is Our Mother Trail
37	Devil's Hole State Park
38	Old Fort Niagara State Historic Site / Beach Trail
39	Letchworth State Park: Lower, Upper, and Middle Falls Area
40	Newtown Battlefield State Park
Best Hikes for Artistic and Literary History	
2	Walt Whitman Trail and Long Island Summit
6	Old Croton Aqueduct Trail: Scarborough to Sleepy Hollow
12	Olana State Historic Site
26	North-South Lake Campground Escarpment Trail Loop
Best Hikes for Industrial History	
6	Old Croton Aqueduct Trail: Scarborough to Sleepy Hollow
7	Walkway Over the Hudson State Historic Park and Loop Trail
11	Taconic State Park: Copake Falls Mine Area and Bash Bish Falls
15	Peebles Island State Park
17	Hooper Garnet Mine
18	OK Slip Falls
21	Tahawus Ghost Town
23	Upper Delaware River / Roebling Bridge
25	Harriman State Park: Iron Mines Loop
27	Onteora Lake / Bluestone Wild Forest
28	Erie Canalway Trail: Warners to Camillus
31	Genesee Riverway Trail and Rochester Lighthouse
32	Erie Canalway Trail: Pittsford to Fairport

Best Hikes for History of the Wealthiest Americans	
4	Sands Point Preserve
5	Rockefeller State Park Preserve
8	Eleanor's Walk and Top Cottage Trail
9	Roosevelt Farm and Forest
10	Vanderbilt Mansion Loop
12	Olana State Historic Site
30	Glimmerglass State Park and Hyde Hall
39	Letchworth State Park: Upper and Middle Falls Area
Best Hikes for Lighthouses	
3	Fire Island Lighthouse
13	Kingston Point Rotary Park
22	Crown Point State Historic Site to Vermont
31	Genesee Riverway Trail and Rochester Lighthouse
38	Old Fort Niagara State Historic Site / Beach Trail

Long Island

The boardwalk at Fire Island Light helps preserve the fragile dunes.

1 Camp Hero State Park

Sand, surf, and the occasional military ordnance are the charms of this coastal hike at the eastern tip of southern Long Island.

Start: Battery 113 Trailhead parking area
Distance: 2.0-mile loop
Hiking time: About 1 hour
Elevation gain: 78 feet
High point: 97 feet
Difficulty: Easy
Best season: Spring through fall
Traffic: Foot, bicycle, and equestrian use

Fees and permits: Fee collected on weekends in May, October, and November; daily from Memorial Day weekend to Columbus Day weekend
Maps: Available online at camphero.net/timeline/statepark
Trail contacts: Camp Hero State Park, 1898 Montauk Hwy., Montauk 11954; (631) 668-3781; nysparks.com/parks/97/details.aspx

Finding the trailhead: On Long Island's south fork, take the Montauk Highway (NY 27) through the town of Montauk and continue toward Montauk Point. Turn right onto Camp Hero Road (you'll see the signs for Camp Hero State Park), and follow the signs to the Battery 113 Trail. GPS: N41 03.800' / W71 52.302'

The Hike

Beginning in a maritime forest, this fairly easy hike leads to some of the best coastal views in New York, with wide expanses of the Atlantic Ocean stretching before your vantage point along high bluffs. The trail also reveals the remains of a military base that protected the eastern seaboard during World War II, where alert observers watched for German boats that might attempt to sneak up on this surreptitiously guarded outpost.

The first third of this hike wanders through woods from one end of the Battery 113 Trail to the other, on a largely unmarked trail crisscrossed with shallow streams. Once it emerges on the park road, this loop continues to the main attraction: sculpted bluffs that rise above a gravelly sand beach, with the sparkling ocean beyond. During the spring and fall migrations and throughout winter, this is an excellent spot from which to scan for Long Island's specialty seabirds: northern gannet, all three species of scoter (white-winged, black, and surf), common and king eiders, red-throated and common loons, and horned and red-necked grebes. You'll see plenty of red-breasted merganser, scaup, long-tailed duck, and other sea-loving birds here as well. American oystercatcher, black skimmer, Forster's tern, and Bonaparte's gull are often numerous here, and you may catch harbor seals sunning themselves on the shore. It's very likely that you will find surfcasting anglers here, enjoying one of the best places in New York to catch striped bass.

Historical Background

As one of the easternmost and most isolated points on the East Coast of the United States, Montauk Point has served as a strategic military outpost since the Revolutionary War. The Battle of Long Island took place here against the British in 1776, and Montauk Lighthouse—not featured on this hike, but visible nearby—provided a lookout for British ships throughout the War of 1812. During World War I, this area rose in importance once again as the military stationed troops and reconnaissance dirigibles here in case of attack. When the United States joined World War II, the US Army's Camp Hero masqueraded as a fishing village, covering its bunkers and batteries with Hollywood-style scenery and standing ready for action should the country be attacked by sea. German U-boats lurked offshore while the US Navy used nearby land to install seaplane hangars, docks, and barracks, as well as a facility for testing torpedoes.

The German attack never came, but Camp Hero remained an active base throughout the 1950s, as the navy withdrew and the army provided part of the land to the 773rd Aircraft Control & Warning Squadron. When the radar tower was installed in 1958, the unit became the SAGE radar squadron, serving at Camp Hero until July 1, 1980. The motors and electronics no longer reside inside the radar tower, but the antenna remains in place as a reminder of more-tenuous times.

That's the official military story, but conspiracy theorists have many other ideas about what may have gone on here. A series of books by author Preston Nichols, who reportedly writes from recovered repressed memories of his involvement at this site, suggest that a series of secret US government experiments took place here under the name The Montauk Project. This research sought to develop techniques of psychological warfare, discover methods of time travel, and perform the first teleportation tests. Those who believe the government faked the 1969 *Apollo* moon landing theorize that it was staged here, and they speculate that the experiments tore a hole in the space-time continuum. Keep an eye open during your hike, because these conspiracy theorists also believe that the government made contact with alien life here. No doubt E.T. will find it easier to phone home now than he did when the 1982 film premiered, as he can use the smartphone technology you have in your pocket.

The Original General Hero

While Camp Hero's name seems entirely appropriate for a military base, it actually takes the moniker from the surname of an army officer. Maj. Gen. Andrew Hero Jr. served in the US Army for many decades, rising in the ranks from second lieutenant in 1891 to his final position as the US Army's chief of coastal artillery in 1926. In his long and distinguished career, Hero served with several artillery regiments and as aide-de-camp to Brig. Gen. Joseph P. Sanger, commander of the District of Matanzas in Cuba. He commanded the 154th Field Artillery Brigade during World War I and went on to command several coast artillery districts before becoming chief of the entire coastal operation. Major General Hero is buried in Arlington National Cemetery.

Hero came from a solid military background. He was the son of Confederate soldier Andrew Hero, who served with the Washington Artillery during the Civil War, first as a second sergeant in 1861 and finally as a captain in 1864. The elder Hero also lived up to his surname, suffering wounds at Sharpsburg in September 1862 and at Petersburg in April 1865, and surviving the Battle of Gettysburg (where a third of the Confederate soldiers were killed, wounded, or missing by the end of the battle).

As you follow the gravel road along the top of the bluff and into an area with increased foliage, watch for red fox, white-tailed deer, eastern cottontail, eastern chipmunk, and both gray and red squirrels. Also keep an eye out for unexploded ordnance (UXO)—while it's not likely that you will come upon a military shell on this well-traveled trail, signs along the way recommend that you report it if you see it.

One of the most impressive landmarks on this hike dates back to the camp's World War II heritage: the Semi-Automatic Ground Environment (SAGE) radar tower used from 1958 until the camp closed in 1980. Here the 773rd Radar Squadron served as part of the national air defense network, doing double duty as part of the NORAD defense system. The radar antenna has been deactivated, but it stands here where it was "abandoned in place" in 1984.

Miles and Directions

0.0   Start from the parking area at the Battery 113 Trailhead and take the trail to the Bluff Overlook. There's only one trail, and blazes/markers are erratic.

The military has left Camp Hero, but the radar tower remains.

Camp Hero State Park

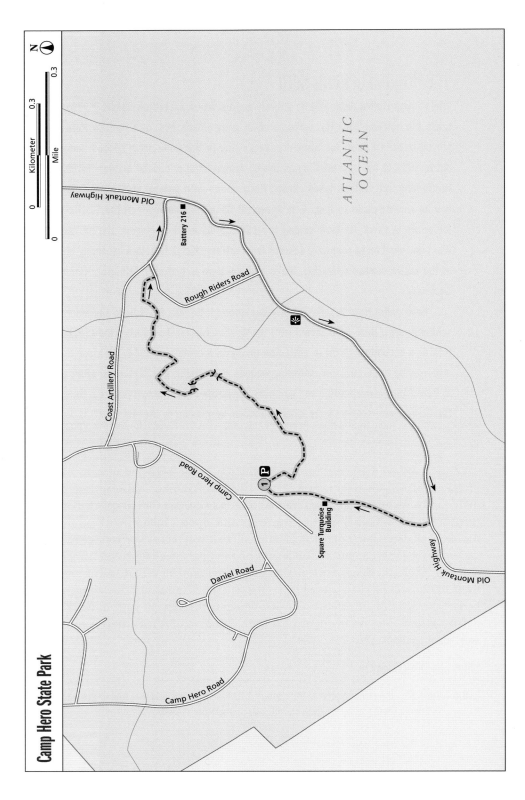

Old Montauk Highway

Battery 216

Rough Riders Road

Coast Artillery Road

Camp Hero Road

Square Turquoise Building

Daniel Road

Camp Hero Road

Old Montauk Highway

ATLANTIC OCEAN

N

Kilometer   0   0.3

Mile   0   0.3

1 P

The batteries at Camp Hero held ammunition in case of a World War II enemy attack.

0.3 Cross a bridge (a real one with railings) over a stream.

0.4 Cross another bridge.

0.5 Cross one more "real" bridge. Reach an intersection and turn right, toward the orange Office of Parks, Recreation, and Historic Preservation marker. Cross one more bridge.

0.7 The Battery 113 Trail ends at the road. Turn left and continue to the main road. Turn right at the barrier. At the next corner (Coast Artillery Road), turn right again.

0.9 Reach the parking area at Battery 216. Here's a bluff with a wide view of the ocean. Pick up the trail to your right as you face the ocean. This wide, gravel trail bends to the left to follow the bluff.

1.3 A break in the foliage at the handicapped parking area provides an overlook of the ocean and bluffs. Access to the rocky beach is permitted for anglers and hikers. You'll see the remains of an old dock here. In another 0.1 mile the gravel road ends; continue straight on the path. This is where you need to watch out for UXOs.

1.6 A paved road goes left. Pass it and continue straight. In a moment the path to the bluff overlook goes left and there's a gate to the right. Continue straight as the road becomes paved.

1.9 There's a square turquoise building on your left. Continue straight.

2.0 Complete the loop at the parking area.

2 Walt Whitman Trail and Long Island Summit

Walk to the highest point on Long Island and see the view that inspired one of the most universally revered poets in American history.

Start: At the end of Reservoir Road in the town of Melville, Suffolk County
Distance: 0.6-mile lollipop
Hiking time: About 30 minutes
Elevation gain: 126 feet
High point: 401 feet
Difficulty: Easy
Best season: Year-round

Traffic: Hikers, joggers, people with dogs
Fees and permits: No fees or permits required
Maps: Available online at mapmyhike.com/us/west-hills-ny
Trail contact: West Hills County Park, Sweet Hollow Road, Melville 11747; (631) 854-4423; suffolkcountyny.gov/Departments/Parks/Parks/WestHillsCountyPark.aspx

Finding the trailhead: From the Northern State Parkway, take exit 40 at Walt Whitman Road. Turn left onto Walt Whiteman Road (NY 110), and bear left on Old Walt Whitman Road. Continue to West Hills Road; turn left. Take the third left onto Reservoir Road. Follow Reservoir Road to its end at the trailhead; park here. GPS: N40 48.990' / W73 25.433'

The Hike

This popular hiking park near Huntington offers an easy walk with just enough change in elevation to prove that Long Island does have its share of hills. The short

Historical Background

In 1819, in a farmhouse in West Hills at what is now 246 Old Walt Whitman Rd., poet Walter Whitman Jr. was born to house builder Walter Whitman and his wife, Louisa. The second of nine children, "Walt"—a nickname he received to differentiate him from his father—moved with his family to Brooklyn four years later. He took his first job at age 12, working for the *Long Island Patriot* newspaper as a "printer's devil," mixing ink and fetching type as he learned the trade. This would lead him into journalism—a profession in which he became an outspoken advocate for social and economic reform—but in his spare time he wrote poetry in a new style he invented, filled with the variations in meter and rhyme that we now call "free verse."

His first book of poems he called *Leaves of Grass*, a thin, self-published volume that did not receive much attention from the general public at the time, though

Reach the summit of Long Island not far from Walt Whitman's birthplace.

segment we've selected is part of the longer (3.8-mile) Walt Whitman Trail, a meander through West Hills County Park in the neighborhood where poet and naturalist
Whitman grew up.

critics praised its innovations in poetic license. Over the course of his life, as Whitman worked for the civil service in the Department of the Interior in Washington and
served as a volunteer nurse throughout the Civil War, his experiences allowed him to
refocus and expand *Leaves of Grass* to the volume studied today in English classes
and read by millions around the world.

Whitman walked the trails in what is now West Hills County Park as a child and
later as an adult, when his parents moved back to this area after their children were
grown. In addition to walking in the poet's footsteps here, you can also visit the Walt
Whitman Birthplace State Historic Site to learn more about the life and times of one
of America's most celebrated writers.

Walt Whitman Trail and Long Island Summit

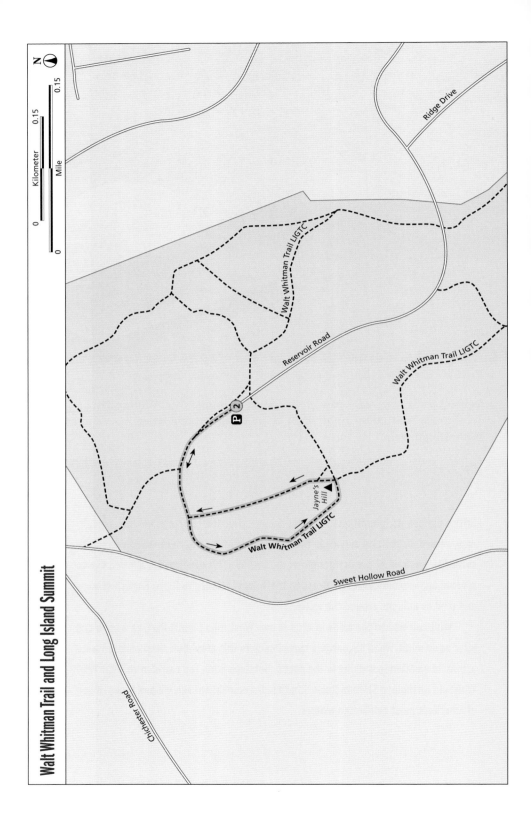

The zenith of this hike comes in at just 401 feet, but it is the highest point on Long Island, providing hikers with a delightful view that may extend for 30 miles or more on a clear day. While the hiking here is good any time of the year, the crisp fall air provides the best opportunities for long-distance viewing.

Miles and Directions

0.0 Start at the end of Reservoir Road. Proceed straight ahead into the woods, past the metal gate and onto the nicely groomed dirt trail. You will see trail markers for the USA National Recreation Trail. When the path forks after the building on your left, take the left fork. Watch for the white blazes and the sign welcoming you to the Walt Whitman Trail.

0.1 Continue to your left. (If you want to explore the whole Walt Whitman Trail, it continues to your right.) Sandy Reservoir appears on your left.

0.3 You have reached Jayne's Hill and the summit of Long Island—the highest point on the island. There's a rock here with a plaque commemorating the spot. When you're ready, face the verse on the rock and take the trail to your right (following the white blazes).

0.5 At the intersection, bear right to complete the loop.

0.6 Arrive back at the end of Reservoir Road.

3 Fire Island Lighthouse

A sturdy boardwalk leads through windswept dunes to a beacon that guided captains and immigrants into New York Harbor for generations.

Start: Robert Moses State Park, parking field #5, at the east end of the lot
Distance: 2.0 miles out and back
Hiking time: About 1 hour
Elevation gain: 29 feet
High point: 26 feet
Difficulty: Easy
Best season: Summer (but open year-round)
Traffic: Hikers only
Fees and permits: During beach season, parking fees are in effect. If you wish to climb to the top of the lighthouse, there's an admission fee there as well.

Maps: Fire Island National Seashore map available online at nps.gov/fiis; click on "View Park Map"
Trail contacts: Fire Island National Seashore, 120 Laurel St., Patchogue 11772; (631) 687-4750; nps.gov/fiis. Fire Island Lighthouse; (631) 321-7028.
Special considerations: Please don't feed the numerous deer, which have become conditioned to beg for food from tourists. Pets are not permitted on this trail. Stay on the boardwalk; the dunes here are fragile.

Finding the trailhead: From I-495 East take exit 38 to the Northern State Parkway. Travel south on the parkway to exit 31A at the Meadowbrook State Parkway. Continue south on this parkway until you reach the Ocean Parkway. Turn east onto the Ocean Parkway and continue to the causeway to Robert Moses State Park. Cross the causeway and continue to Fire Island Inlet Bridge in Robert Moses State Park. Follow the signs to the end of the parking area and the boardwalk to the lighthouse. GPS: N40 37.732' / W73 13.751'

The Hike

On this narrow strip of land with the Atlantic Ocean on either side, Fire Island Lighthouse braves the elements and invites visitors to climb to the top of its tower for stunning views of the maritime landscape. Part of Fire Island National Seashore, a unit of the National Park Service, this lighthouse and its uncommonly pleasant boardwalk trail give hikers a sampling of all that is good about the park service: gorgeous views, meticulous historic preservation, enthusiastic interpretation of artifacts and buildings, and respect for the natural flora and fauna with which we share our remaining open spaces.

You may encounter deer that are much more forward than is good for them, as well as dozens of bird species—the most common of which include herring gulls, yellow warblers, gray catbirds, eastern towhees, song sparrows, and barn, tree, rough-winged, and bank swallows vying for airspace with red-winged blackbirds

The original Fresnel lens is on display in the Fire Island museum. ▶

Historical Background

A lighthouse has stood on Fire Island since 1826, guiding transatlantic ships into New York Harbor and welcoming immigrants from all over Europe to America. The current light, shining across the harbor since 1858, used a first-order Fresnel lens that flashed once each minute, powered by whale or mineral oil. In 1938 electricity arrived at Fire Island Light—though on the day scheduled for the lighthouse to glow with electric light for the first time, a hurricane struck the island and wiped out the connection.

In 1915 the US Coast Guard established a station here on Fire Island, and management of the light became the responsibility of the US Lighthouse Service. When Congress dissolved the Lighthouse Service in 1939 "in the interest of economy and efficiency," the Coast Guard managed the station until decommissioning the light in 1973. A small light on the Robert Moses State Park water tower now guides boats into New York Harbor, but Fire Island Light continues as a landmark under the protection of the National Park Service, with the invaluable assistance of the Fire Island Lighthouse Preservation Society. The society took on the job of restoring the lighthouse, raising $1.3 million in 1984 to restore it to its 1939 condition.

and common grackles. The coastal scrubland provides a range of plants that thrive in sandy, windswept places like this one. Look for woolly beach heather, beach plum, northern bayberry, beach grass, and Virginia creeper—and keep an eye out for poison ivy.

Once you reach the lighthouse, you are welcome (for a fee) to climb the 182 steps to the top of the tower. It's worth the price of admission to enjoy the view from the top, including the best view you'll find anywhere of the entire national seashore extending eastward.

Miles and Directions

0.0 Start at the trailhead at the east end of parking field #5. You can see the lighthouse from here.

0.3 Cross the road and continue straight on the trail to the lighthouse. If you'd prefer to stop at the observation tower, turn left here.

0.6 The boardwalk to the right goes to the beach. The lighthouse is right in front of you here. Follow the gentle incline to the lighthouse station, where you can see the original Fresnel lens.

Fire Island Lighthouse

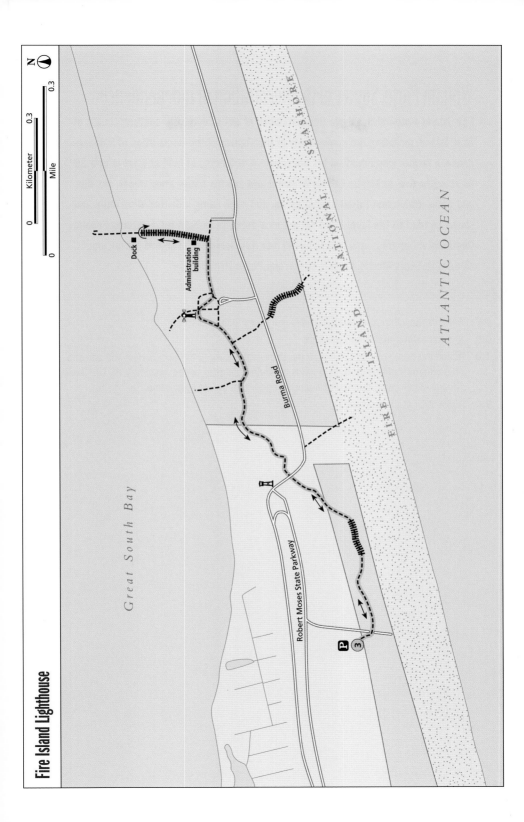

N

Kilometer
0   0.3

Mile
0   0.3

Great South Bay

Dock

Administration
building

Burma Road

Robert Moses State Parkway

P
3

FIRE ISLAND NATIONAL SEASHORE

ATLANTIC OCEAN

William Floyd, Signer of the Declaration of Independence

Fire Island National Seashore has a number of units along the southern coast of Long Island, including the home of one of the signers of the Declaration of Independence. A farmer who inherited his house and 4,400 acres of land at what is now 20 Washington Ave. in Mastic Beach, William Floyd and his family grew wheat, rye, flax, and other grains and raised sheep, cattle, and pigs, using indentured servants and slaves to tend to the land. Floyd served as a delegate in both the First and Second Continental Congress, and he was one of four New Yorkers who signed the document, along with Lewis Morris, Francis Lewis, and Philip Livingston.

0.7 Arrive at the lighthouse. The boardwalk continues to the left.

0.9 Turn left toward the lighthouse dock.

1.0 Reach the boathouse at the end of the dock, with a view of the ocean. Here you can see an authentic surf boat and other kinds of equipment used by the legendary US Life-Saving Service. When you are ready, turn around and return the way you came.

2.0 Arrive back at the trailhead.

4 Sands Point Preserve

Discover a castle on the edge of Long Island Sound and see the view formerly reserved for the richest people in New York.

Start: Trailhead in the parking area at Sands Point
Distance: 0.8-mile lollipop
Hiking time: About 30 minutes
Elevation gain: 81 feet
High point: 89 feet
Difficulty: Easy
Best season: Spring through fall; mid-June for the bloom of 1,500 red rose bushes

Traffic: Hikers, joggers, fitness enthusiasts
Fees and permits: Entry fee per car
Maps: Available online at thesandspointpreserve.com/sands-point-trail-map-for-printing
Trail contacts: Friends of the Sands Point Preserve, 127 Middle Neck Rd., Sands Point 10050; (516) 571-7901; thesandspoint preserve.com

Finding the trailhead: From the Long Island Expressway (LIE), going east, take exit 36 (Searingtown Road/Port Washington). Turn left at the light and take Searingtown Road north (this becomes Port Washington Boulevard and then Middle Neck Road). Watch for the preserve on your right.

From the LIE going west, take exit 36 and make a right at the light; follow the directions above. GPS: N40 51.682' / W73 41.913'

The Hike

This hike follows a fitness trail—outfitted with exercise stations and instructions—through a corner of the 216-acre estate once owned by the son of a railroad tycoon and later by mining magnate Daniel Guggenheim and his wife, Florence. You will begin your hike in front of Hempstead House, the least "house"-like structure you may see this year. The unmistakable castle design hearkens back to the Tudor era, a testament to the fabulous wealth its owners enjoyed. Behind the castle, more than 1,500 rose bushes bloom deep red in June, and fountains add elegance and old-world character.

While there are other trails on the grounds, the one we chose takes you to one of the most expansive and comprehensive views of Long Island Sound that you will find along the island's north coast. From the cliffs you can see exactly what attracted some of the most wealthy people in America to choose this area as their home—and why F. Scott Fitzgerald made northern Long Island's "Gold Coast" the setting of his masterpiece of fiction, *The Great Gatsby*.

This walk leads through a successional forest in which you may spot groundhogs, chipmunks, and squirrels scurrying beneath falling leaves, and to the outskirts of a meadow where deer may come to feed early in the morning or in the last moments

Historical Background

Who builds a 50,000-foot mansion for his own personal use? Howard Gould, the son of railroad mogul Jay Gould, commissioned this one in 1912 and lived here with his wife, Katherine Clemmons. Designed by architects Hunt & Hunt, the 226-foot-long, 128-foot-wide castle features a foyer that extends 60 feet upward, which in turn houses a recently restored Wurlitzer Opus 445 theatre organ. The furnishings used by the Goulds—and the Guggenheims, who purchased the home in 1917—were removed after Daniel Guggenheim died in 1930, but visitors can still see the library with its walnut paneling copied from the palace of King James I of England and its ceiling adorned with plaster-relief portraits of literary figures. A visit to the summer living room reveals stone gargoyles around the ceiling, and other rooms bring in natural light through tall Gothic windows.

While Florence Guggenheim had the mansion sealed when she moved out after Daniel's death, Hempstead House reopened in 1940 to provide a home to seventy-five British refugee children during World War II. Two years later, Mrs. Guggenheim donated the castle to the Institute of Aeronautical Sciences, and in 1946 it became the property of the US Navy, which used it as a training center. Nassau County acquired it for use as a park in 1967 along with 128 acres of the property, receiving the remaining 80 acres as a bequest in the will of Harry Guggenheim, the son of Daniel and Florence. Today this property is maintained by the Friends of Sands Point Preserve.

Two other mansions on the property are not as opulent as Hempstead House, but they are more than noteworthy. Florence Guggenheim had Mille Fleurs built for her after Daniel's passing, downsizing her space and belongings for her later years. Falasie, the mansion on the beach built in 1923 for Harry Guggenheim and his wife, Caroline Morton, resembles a thirteenth-century Norman manor house and is still furnished with antiques from the sixteenth and seventeenth centuries. You can tour Falasie for a per-person fee in addition to the parking fee.

◄ *The fabulously wealthy Guggenheims lived in this castle in the early 20th century.*

Sands Point Preserve

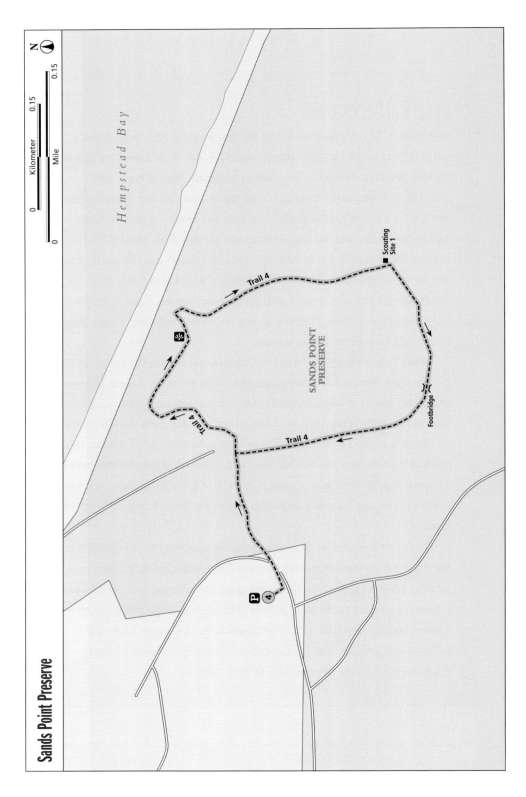

Hempstead Bay

SANDS POINT
PRESERVE

Trail 4

Trail 4

Trail 4

Scouting
Site 1

Footbridge

P

4

Kilometer
0   0.15   0.15

Mile
0   0.15

N

Stop to admire the view of Long Island Sound from Sands Point.

of sunset. Birds abound in this coastal habitat, especially during spring and fall, when these woods become a stopover before and after migrating flocks cross the sound.

Miles and Directions

0.0 Start from the parking area and go toward the paved road next to the castle. Head downhill. Cross the bridge over the pond, and go straight through the trail intersection to take Trail 4.

0.1 Turn left onto Trail 4.

0.2 At the intersection with Trail 8, continue on Trail 4. Watch on your left for an unmarked path to a great view of the shoreline of Long Island Sound. Watch your step—there's no barrier here.

0.3 Here's an even better overlook from the cliff.

0.4 At the intersection with Trail 6, continue straight on Trail 4.

0.5 Reach Scouting Site 1, where you'll see picnic tables and a fire pit. Facing the intersection, take the path to the right.

0.6 Go under the footbridge. In a moment, the trail intersects Trail 6. Continue straight to the beginning of the loop; turn left to return to the parking area.

0.8 Arrive back at the parking area.

Hudson River Valley

Pass a healthy pond ecosystem on your way to the Copake Iron Works.

5 Rockefeller State Park Preserve

Walk the carriage roads that John D. Rockefeller Jr. created on his own land for the enjoyment of the local and global community.

Start: Visitor center at 125 Phelps Way in Pleasantville
Distance: 3.7-mile lollipop
Hiking time: About 2 hours
Elevation gain: 159 feet
High point: 308 feet
Difficulty: Moderate
Best season: Spring and fall

Traffic: Hikers, joggers, cyclists, equestrians, cross-country skiers
Fees and permits: Parking fee
Maps: Available online at nysparks.com/parks/attachments/RockefellerTrailMap.pdf
Trail contacts: Rockefeller State Park Preserve, 125 Phelps Way, Pleasantville 10570; (914) 631-1470; nysparks.com/parks/59/details.aspx

Finding the trailhead: From US 95 South, take NY 287 West (Cross Westchester Expressway) toward the Tappan Zee Bridge. Take exit 3 for the Sprain Parkway/Taconic Parkway. Keep left on the exit toward the north. Continue on the Sprain Parkway for about 3 miles as it merges onto the Taconic Parkway. Take the Pleasantville exit onto NY 117, and turn left at the end of the ramp to continue on NY 117 West. After the second traffic light, the park appears on your left in about 1 mile. GPS: N41 06.710' / W73 50.237'

The Hike

Few paths are more walkable than those created by John D. Rockefeller Jr., whether they crisscross the lake-strewn landscape between the mountains of Acadia National Park in Maine or wander through the floodplains of the Hudson River Valley. Here at the state park that bears his name, Rockefeller put his love of the outdoors and open space to work to create a parklike setting for his family and his community, and it's our good fortune to be able to come here and wander to our heart's content.

The trail we selected begins with the Old Sleepy Hollow Road Trail, and takes advantage of some connector trails to bring you to the Pocantico Hills, an area of healthy forest and undulating terrain. It then loops back on the Thirteen Bridges Trail, following the Pocantico River to the Eagle Hill Trail, and finally connecting back to the Old Sleepy Hollow Road to bring you up the hill to the visitor center and parking area.

More than 55 miles of carriage roads meander through the Rockefeller estate, so if you'd like to enjoy more of the park than we have featured here, you will find maps and trail descriptions at the visitor center as you enter the park.

Historical Background

There was a time in American history when the immensely rich felt a significant responsibility to do good works with their wealth, creating programs and places that improved the quality of life for a community, a region, or the whole country. John D. Rockefeller Sr. was not the first man in history to make such a commitment to the use of his wealth, but he was one of the first in America to do so—and he set a standard that encouraged many of his fellow business magnates to do the same.

Rockefeller made his money as one of the founders of Standard Oil, revolutionizing the petroleum industry and becoming the first billionaire in American history. With the opportunity to use his fortune for the betterment of mankind, he spent the last forty years of his life here at the estate he called Kykuit, creating a system for philanthropy, establishing foundations, and making gifts that would transform medicine, scientific research, and education.

John Senior had five children, one of whom was John D. Rockefeller Jr., known as "Junior" in most biographies to distinguish him from his father. Junior shared many of his father's philanthropic passions, but he developed his own interest in conservation, becoming one of the great champions of the formation of national parks, including Grand Teton, Acadia, Great Smoky Mountains, Shenandoah, and Yosemite. (The John D. Rockefeller Jr. Parkway between Grand Teton and Yellowstone National Parks was named in his honor after his death.)

Here at home, Junior worked closely with contractors and developers to create the carriage roads throughout the Rockefeller property, opening them to the public on the day they were completed. He acquired many surrounding properties to preserve them for the local community, investing as much as $12 million in the project. Among these are Philipsburg Manor House in North Tarrytown, Sunnyside—home of author Washington Irving, who wrote "The Legend of Sleepy Hollow"—and Van Cortland Manor in Croton-on-Hudson.

Kykuit, the famous four-story mansion at 200 Lake Rd., remains a National Historic Landmark and a property of the National Trust for Historic Preservation. Historic Hudson Valley, the organization founded by Junior (as Sleepy Hollow Restorations) for the stewardship of the historic buildings he acquired, now offers tours of Kykuit for a fee. Information on tours is available at hudsonvalley.org.

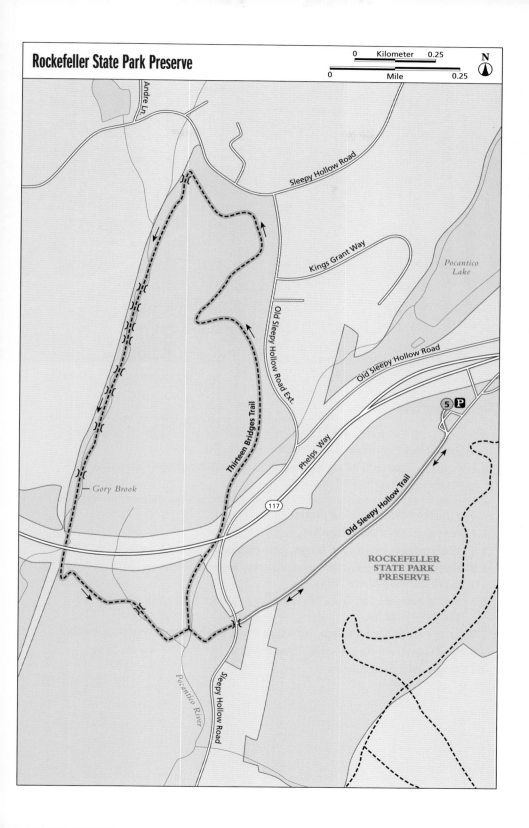

Rockefeller State Park Preserve

Andre Ln

Sleepy Hollow Road

Kings Grant Way

Pocantico Lake

Old Sleepy Hollow Road Ext.

Old Sleepy Hollow Road

Thirteen Bridges Trail

5 P

Gory Brook

Phelps Way

Old Sleepy Hollow Trail

117

ROCKEFELLER
STATE PARK
PRESERVE

Pocantico River

Sleepy Hollow Road

N

0   Kilometer   0.25

0   Mile   0.25

The carriage roads at Rockefeller Park and Preserve offer some of the state's most pleasant hiking.

Miles and Directions

0.0   Start at the trailhead for the Old Sleepy Hollow Road Trail, at the southeast corner of the parking area. Proceed down the wide path.

0.4   Pass the junction with the Ash Tree Loop to the left; continue straight. Nature's Way trail appears on the right; continue straight.

0.6   Cross NY 117 and continue straight. In a moment, cross a bridge and then turn right onto Pocantico Road (which is not marked).

1.4   Turn right onto Thirteen Bridges Trail.

1.8   Reach the first of the thirteen bridges. These continue for the next 0.7 mile.

2.5   Here is the last of the bridges. Continue past the connector path to the Old Croton Aqueduct Trail and cross under NY 117.

2.7   Turn right onto the Gory Brook Trail, and go up a switchback to Eagle Hill Trail. Continue straight on Eagle Hill.

2.8   Cross a bridge. At the three-way intersection ahead, turn left onto the Pocantico River Trail.

3.0   Meet back up with the Old Sleepy Hollow Road Trail, and return the way you came.

3.7   Arrive back at the parking area.

The Legacy of John D. Rockefeller Jr.

While John Rockefeller Sr. devoted much of his life to amassing his fortune, his son, John D. Rockefeller Jr., had the pleasure of putting that fortune to use through charitable giving. "Junior" worked with Frederick Gates, one of the family's advisors, to establish a range of organizations for the public good: the Rockefeller Institute for Medical Research, the General Education Board, the Sanitary Commission for the Eradication of Hookworm, and the family's foundation. When Junior rose in the public eye, his father transferred a large share of his fortune to his son directly, giving Junior the freedom to contribute to the causes of his choice. The younger Rockefeller bought vast acreages of land and turned them over to the National Park Service, creating Grand Teton National Park and paying for the construction of 57 miles of carriage roads that would become part of Acadia National Park in Maine. His efforts helped build a museum in Yosemite National Park, and he purchased the land for Humboldt Redwoods State Park in California. In all, he gave more than $45 million to land conservation, making him one of the top open-space philanthropists to this day.

Junior also took an interest in historic preservation, providing the funds that created Colonial Williamsburg from a handful of crumbling buildings and funding the restoration of the thirteenth-century French cathedral Notre-Dame de Reims after it was nearly demolished by shellfire in World War I. He gave a large sum to the restoration of Versailles, the palace constructed for Louis XIV in France, and provided the funds for archaeological excavation of the Ancient Agora of Athens. Closer to home, Junior became personally involved in the creation of The Cloisters, the medieval abbey–style art museum in uptown Manhattan, funding the acquisition and transport of parts of five abbeys in France to be used in the construction of the lavish museum.

In all, historians believe that John D. Rockefeller Jr. gave upwards of $537 million to philanthropic causes, nearly matching his father's contributions of $540 million. To this day, the family stands as one of the most generous in American history.

6 Old Croton Aqueduct Trail: Scarborough to Sleepy Hollow

Follow the course of New York City's original water source on a shady trail with generous dashes of history.

Start: River Road in Briarcliff Manor
Distance: 3.6-mile shuttle or 7.2 miles out and back
Hiking time: About 1.5 hours one way; 3 hours round-trip
Elevation gain: 295 feet
High point: 182 feet
Difficulty: Easy
Best season: Apr through Nov

Traffic: Trail runners, cross-country skiers, cyclists, equestrians
Fees and permits: No fees or permits required
Maps: Available for purchase from Friends of the Old Croton Aqueduct Inc., (914) 693-4117, or at aqueduct.org
Trail contact: Old Croton Aqueduct State Historic Park, 15 Walnut St., Dobbs Ferry 10522; (914) 693-5259 or (914) 631-1470; nysparks.com/parks/96/details.aspx

Finding the trailhead: From the north or south, take the New York Thruway (I-87 North) to exit 9 (Tarrytown/Sleepy Hollow/US 9 North). Travel north on US 9 for 4.6 miles to River Road in Briarcliff Manor. Turn left onto River Road and park in the parking area to the left of the road across from Scarborough School. GPS: N41 07.832' / W73 51.671'
Shuttle drop-off: To reach the second parking area at the end of the hike, from exit 9 on I-87, travel north on US 9 to Bedford Road in Sleepy Hollow. Turn right onto Bedford Road and continue to the Old Croton Aqueduct State Historic Park parking area. GPS: N41 05.212' / W73 51.35'

The Hike

One of the area's oldest and most established walking trails, the Old Croton Aqueduct Trail connects the Lower Hudson Valley with Yonkers and the Bronx by following the route of New York City's first transported water supply. Your hike takes you atop the protective covering of earth that shields the aqueduct from the elements, allowing this remarkable feat of engineering to carry clean water from Croton Dam all the way to the center of New York, where it filled reservoirs on the sites of today's Great Lawn in Central Park and the New York Public Library.

Old Croton Aqueduct was retired in 1965 (although parts of it still bring water to Ossining), but its subterranean passageways still stand. The surface level served as an informal walkway for local and long-distance pedestrians throughout the aqueduct's history. Today Old Croton Aqueduct State Historic Park provides excellent strolling, cycling, and hiking to tens of thousands of area residents each year.

Historical Background

With the population of New York City growing exponentially in the 1830s as hundreds of thousands of immigrants arrived from overseas, the nation's largest city had become a sanitation nightmare and a hotbed of waste-borne diseases. Native Americans had found plenty of freshwater in springs on the island of Manhattan, but the use of these water sources by industrial companies in the 1800s led to pollution not only of the springs but also of cisterns and wells dug to support eighteenth-century European settlers.

By 1830 the city struggled to access freshwater from any source, and the annual mortality rate within the metropolis had risen to 2.6 percent, or one in every thirty-nine people. Yellow fever was the greatest killer until 1832, when cholera arrived and sent the death rate skyrocketing. Areas like Five Points, one of the most notorious slums in the world, saw thousands of people die because of the poor sanitary conditions—a deplorable situation, but one that could be corrected by bringing an abundant supply of clean freshwater into the heart of the city.

The last straw came in December 1835, when the Great Fire of New York destroyed 17 city blocks and caused $20 million in property damage—an astronomical sum in the early nineteenth century—because both the East and Hudson Rivers were frozen solid and no other source of water was available to quench the fire. Money talked louder than public hardship, and in 1837 construction began on an aqueduct that would bring water from upstate lakes into the city.

The Croton Aqueduct brings water through an 8.5-foot-high iron pipe from the Croton Dam, dropping 13 inches per mile for 41 miles to transport water using only the force of gravity. Ventilating towers keep the water fresh within the pipe (you'll pass three of these on this hike), and hydraulic cement allows the aqueduct to cross the Harlem River and other waterways on its way south.

Your hike crosses the Archville Bridge, which reconnected segments of the trail after a seventy-four-year severance. Perhaps best of all, you will pass through Sleepy Hollow—a real place after all—where author Washington Irving penned his classic tale of Ichabod Crane and the Headless Horseman. Irving's remains are interred in the Sleepy Hollow Cemetery (as are those of legendary industrialist and philanthropist Andrew Carnegie), a stop worthy of a detour from the main trail.

Miles and Directions

0.0 Start from the parking area on River Road in Scarborough and begin walking south on the aqueduct trail. The path is mowed here, with a narrow, bare dirt trail running down the middle. There's a neighborhood just beyond the wooded area to your right.

0.2 Reach ventilator #10.

0.4 Note the trail markers (the first you've seen) here. These are the State of New York Taconic region markers, white plastic disks with black ink. The trail turns right here; you'll walk a short paved portion past a private home. Soon the trail bears left across this private property. Continue on the trail to Country Club Road. Cross the road and continue straight on the trail.

0.8 A connecting trail goes right here. Bear left. The trail becomes a wide, crushed-stone path through a lovely wooded area. You'll see many Japanese wineberry bushes along the trail. These bear fruit in July; you're welcome to sample.

0.9 Arrive at the Archville Bridge. A stone marker here notes that the aqueduct's first arch over a road—Broadway in this case—was completed here in 1839. In a moment you'll come to ventilator #11.

1.8 A loop trail goes to the left here. Follow the green signposts for the "OCA" and turn right. Cross the bridge over NY 117. After the bridge, take the first trail to your right. You're now

Ventilators are prominent landmarks along the Old Croton Aqueduct Trail.

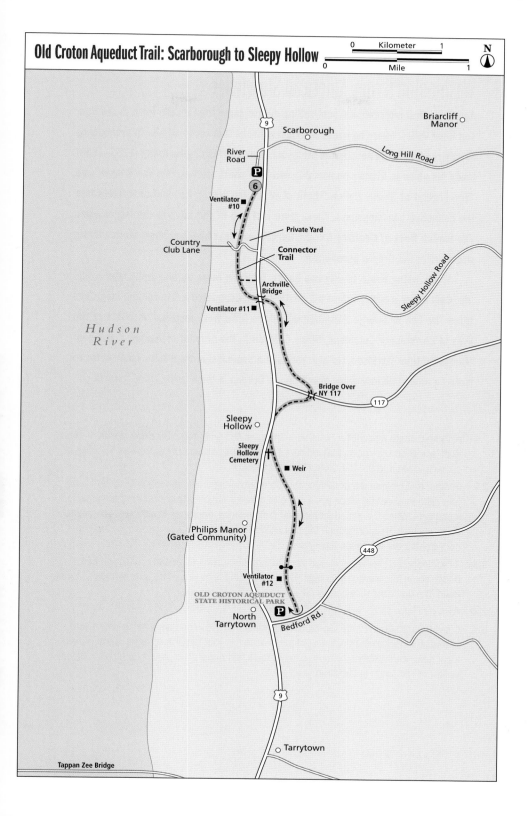

Old Croton Aqueduct Trail: Scarborough to Sleepy Hollow

Kilometer

Mile

N

Briarcliff
Manor

Scarborough

Long Hill Road

River
Road

P

6

Ventilator
#10

Private Yard

Country
Club Lane

**Connector
Trail**

Archville
Bridge

Ventilator #11 ■

*Hudson
River*

Sleepy Hollow Road

Bridge Over
NY 117

117

Sleepy
Hollow

Sleepy
Hollow
Cemetery

■ Weir

Philips Manor
(Gated Community)

448

Ventilator
#12

OLD CROTON AQUEDUCT
STATE HISTORICAL PARK

P

North
Tarrytown

Bedford Rd.

9

Tappan Zee Bridge

Tarrytown

Washington Irving, American Storyteller

America's first international best-selling author came from a little town in the Hudson River Valley, where he wrote stories and books that rocketed him to prominence among readers in the new United States and abroad. Washington Irving (1783–1859) made his place in literary immortality with two short stories, "Rip Van Winkle" and "The Legend of Sleepy Hollow," both of which put iconic fictional characters into the collective consciousness. These were just two of the tales in the larger book, *The Sketch Book of Geoffrey Crayon, Gent*, one of four books of short stories Irving wrote under the Crayon pseudonym.

In all, Irving wrote twenty-two books, focusing more on biography later in his life. Only a few months before his death, Irving completed a five-volume biography titled *The Life of George Washington*, and his life's work included accounts of the lives of Christopher Columbus, Oliver Goldsmith, the prophet Mohammed, and poet Margaret Miller Davidson. He also received a commission from John Jacob Astor to write an official history of his expedition to Oregon, a tome Irving titled *Astoria*.

passing through Rockefeller State Park Preserve. Access to the preserve is free from here. You'll see short blue posts that indicate intersections between the preserve's 55 miles of carriage roads and the Old Croton Aqueduct Trail.

2.7 Another trail crosses the aqueduct trail. Continue straight. Sleepy Hollow Cemetery is on your right. In about 50 steps you'll come to a weir, a large masonry edifice that contains a metal gate. When the aqueduct required maintenance, operators could lower the gate to divert the flow of water through the tunnel. Weirs were used at river crossings—the aqueduct crosses the Pocantico River here.

3.3 As you approach the wrought-iron gate ahead, the Hudson River and the Tappan Zee Bridge come into view on your right. Pass around the right side of the gate and cross Brook Road. The trail continues across the street.

3.4 Pass ventilator #12.

3.6 Cross Bedford Road to the Old Croton Aqueduct State Historic Park parking area. If you are walking back to the beginning of the hike, this is your turnaround point. If you parked a car here, your hike has come to an end. You'll find many good places for lunch in Sleepy Hollow or just south in Tarrytown.

7 Walkway Over the Hudson State Historic Park and Loop Trail

Cross a brilliantly repurposed railroad bridge high above the Hudson River, and cross back on the Mid-Hudson Bridge for some of the valley's most spectacular views.

Start: Off of Parker Ave.; set GPS for 60 Parker Ave.
Distance: 4.2-mile loop
Hiking time: About 2.5 hours
Elevation gain: 363 feet
High point: 234 feet
Difficulty: Moderate
Best season: Apr through Nov
Traffic: Joggers, families with strollers, dog walkers, people in wheelchairs, cyclists, in-line skaters
Fees and permits: No fees or permits required

Maps: Walkway Over the Hudson State Historic Park, walkway.org
Trail contact: New York State Office of Parks, Recreation, and Historic Preservation; (845) 834-2867; nysparks.com/parks/178/details.aspx
Special considerations: The concrete walkway can be very hot in summer, with little or no shade. If you bring your dog, bring a water bowl and water, and be ready to carry a small dog if the pavement becomes too hot. No skateboards are permitted.

Finding the trailhead: The parking area is at 60 Parker Ave. in Poughkeepsie. Traveling south on US 9 from Hyde Park, turn left at the junction with NY 9G and follow 9G until it becomes Parker Avenue. The parking lot is on the left in about 0.2 mile.

Traveling north on US 9, turn right onto NY 55 in Poughkeepsie and take US 44/NY 55 North at Washington Street. Continue north on Washington to Parker Avenue, and turn right. The parking lot is on the left in about 0.2 mile. GPS: N41 42.749' / W73 55.585'

The Hike

If you only hike one trail in the Hudson River Valley, the Walkway Over the Hudson may be the one for you. Whether you choose to hike the entire loop or you simply walk out onto the former Poughkeepsie-Highland Railroad Bridge to take in the amazing river views, you will have no finer opportunity to appreciate the Hudson River and its beautiful valley than from this vantage point.

The wide, smooth, modern walkway opened on October 3, 2009, and now stands as the longest elevated pedestrian bridge in the world. Visitors can stroll 212 feet above the river's surface and admire a spectacular view of the river to the north and south. A sunny summer Sunday can draw thousands of people to the park, making downtown Poughkeepsie a new meeting place for neighbors and friends throughout the Hudson River Valley.

Recognizing the value of a longer walk for energetic hikers, the state park has designated a loop trail that crosses this bridge and the Mid-Hudson Bridge about 0.5

Historical Background

An inspired repurposing of an industrial bridge, the Walkway Over the Hudson puts back into use a nineteenth-century railroad bridge that served as a major rail corridor for many decades. The Poughkeepsie-Highland Railroad Bridge was the longest bridge in the world when it opened on January 1, 1889—a $3.6-million project that was the first to cross the Hudson River between New York City and Albany. Freight trains carrying iron and lumber, passenger trains from as far north as Boston and heading as far south as Washington, and so-called "rapid transit" trolley cars filled with tourists and students all passed over this bridge. Over the years, the bridge saw livestock, circus trains, and even football fans on their way to and from West Point cross the Hudson on its expanse. At the bridge's peak usage, more than 3,500 rail cars crossed it every day.

When fire severely damaged the bridge in 1974, the remains of the old structure stood dormant until a group of enthusiastic citizens came together with state and federal governments to repair the bridge and transform it into a new state park. The $38.8-million project was actually less expensive than demolishing the damaged bridge—an effort that would have required $50 million to complete. Today the park contains the world's longest pedestrian bridge, 1.28 miles, at a height of 212 feet above the Hudson River.

mile south. A highly trafficked segment of US 44 and NY 55, the Mid–Hudson Bridge has a pedestrian walkway and an attraction of its own: Bridge Music, the remarkable accomplishment of composer Joseph Bertolozzi. The sounds of traffic crossing the bridge inspired Bertolozzi to write a series of pieces that can be described as percussive funk, created using only the sounds he could generate by making the bridge itself his drum kit. You can listen to a wide selection of these jazzy pieces when you reach the Mid–Hudson Bridge arches, where you will find speakers and buttons to push to hear Bertolozzi's Bridge Music.

Miles and Directions

0.0 Start from the parking area; the walkway leads west. Pass through shady woods and over a Poughkeepsie neighborhood before the bridge begins to cross the river. You'll find food concessions here. Once you're on the bridge, the walk across the bridge continues for 1.28 miles.

1.5 The bridge ends here. The walkway continues to your left (southwest) on a paved path. There's parking on this side of the bridge as well. Turn left at the end of the parking area, and continue to walk down the access road. US 44 and NY 55 are on your right.

2.1 At the end of the access road, you'll find Johnson-Iorio Memorial Park. There's a parking area here with interpretive signage about the Mid-Hudson Bridge. Turn left onto the bridge's pedestrian walkway. You're separated from the car traffic by guardrails and steel grating.

2.2 Reach the first Bridge Music listening post, on the first arch. You'll also see signs here about peregrine falcons nesting on this arch; if you're here between February and June, keep an eye out for peregrines flying around this post.

2.5 The second arch has another listening post. You're welcome to linger on the bridge, admire the view, and listen to the music for as long as you like.

2.8 At the end of the bridge, turn left on the walkway trail. The route will be obvious; the sidewalk is fenced here and descends to street level. When you reach Rinaldi Boulevard, turn left.

2.9 Turn right on Main Street. At this corner, there's a plaza with several restaurants, adjacent to Poughkeepsie Station's pedestrian walkway. You may want to stop here for lunch, ice cream, or a smoothie. When you're ready, continue to the covered pedestrian walkway and

An ingenious repurposing of an old railroad bridge led to the creation of this unusual linear park in Poughkeepsie.

Walkway Over the Hudson State Historic Park and Loop Trail

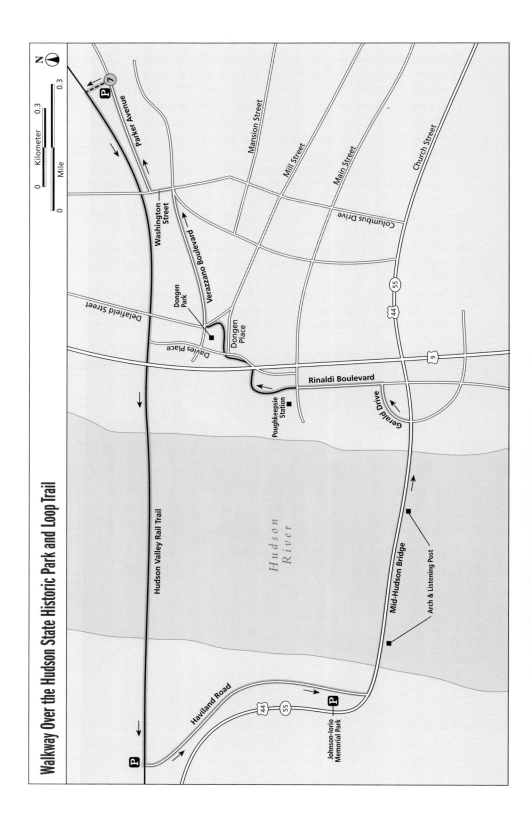

turn left onto the walkway. Continue into the station and turn right. Pass the ticket counter and snack bar and come out on the east side of the station. Continue north on the sidewalk to Davies Place.

3.0 Reach Dongen Park; turn right onto Dongen Place. Continue through the park to Mill Street.

3.3 Turn left onto Mill Street and continue to Verazzano Boulevard. Turn right onto Verazzano.

3.4 Turn left onto Washington Street.

3.8 Turn right onto Parker Avenue and continue to the parking area.

4.2 Arrive back at the parking area.

Views from the Walkway Over the Hudson show Poughkeepsie at its best.

8 Eleanor's Walk and Top Cottage Trail

Hike through the forest planted on orders from President Franklin Roosevelt, and follow the swath cut by the twentieth century's strongest and most influential First Lady.

Start: To the right after you cross the bridge at Eleanor Roosevelt National Historic Site in Hyde Park, on your way to the visitor center and Val-Kill
Distance: 3.1 miles out and back
Hiking time: About 1.5 hours
Elevation gain: 238 feet
High point: 436 feet
Difficulty: Moderate
Best season: Spring through fall

Traffic: Hikers only
Fees and permits: None to hike the trail; fee to tour Val-Kill
Maps: Available online at nps.gov/elro/plan yourvisit/things2do.htm
Trail contacts: The Roosevelt-Vanderbilt National Historic Sites, 4097 Albany Post Rd., Hyde Park 12538; (845) 229-9115, ext. 2010; nps.gov/elro

Finding the trailhead: From the New York State Thruway (I-87), take exit 18 for New Paltz. Take NY 299 east to US 9W South, and follow the signs to the Mid-Hudson Bridge (FDR Bridge). Cross the bridge and follow the signs to US 9 North. Drive 3 miles on US 9 North until you see the Culinary Institute of America (CIA). At the first traffic light after the CIA, turn right onto St. Andrews Road. When St. Andrews ends, turn left onto NY 9G North. Drive 0.5 mile to the entrance to Val-Kill. Park in the lot before the bridge to the visitor center and Val-Kill cottage. The address is 54 Valkill Park Rd., Hyde Park. GPS: N41 45.702' / W73 54.015'

The Hike

It's not every day that you can walk in the footsteps of a First Lady of the United States, so we urge you to seize the opportunity here at Val-Kill. This is the cottage at which Eleanor Roosevelt, wife of President Franklin Delano Roosevelt, pursued her many humanitarian causes and entertained world leaders who came to pay their respects at the grave of her husband. Mrs. Roosevelt walked often in the woods near her cottage, making this a place to contemplate the extraordinary achievements of the woman whom President Harry Truman called "First Lady of the World."

The loop trail called Eleanor's Walk offers a vigorous stroll through healthy woodland, with a small but noticeable change in elevation as you approach a pond. Once you've completed the short loop, we recommend continuing on the Top Cottage Trail, a challenging uphill hike to the house FDR had constructed so he could "escape the mob" of favor-seekers who crowded his calendar throughout his presidency. FDR himself drove his car up this winding road to Top Cottage—back when this road was passable by car. The owner of the adjacent land declined to allow the National Park

Historical Background

The two small houses at this historic site tell us a great deal about the relationship between Franklin and Eleanor Roosevelt before and during FDR's presidency. Val-Kill, constructed on land Franklin gave his wife as a gift, became the home Eleanor shared on weekends with her friends and political coworkers Nancy Cook and Marion Dickerman beginning in 1925. Here Eleanor could get some separation from her domineering mother-in-law and pursue her own interests, including Val-Kill Industries, a manufacturing business in which farmworkers learned marketable skills by making furniture, woven pieces, and pewter household items. When Eleanor became First Lady in 1933, she maintained Val-Kill and its manufacturing buildings as a place to carry on her work whenever she visited Hyde Park—and here she entertained heads of state including British Prime Minister Winston Churchill, the Netherlands' Queen Wilhelmina, First Secretary of the Communist Party of the Soviet Union Nikita Krushchev, Ethiopian Emperor Haile Selassie, Yugoslavian chairman Josip Broz Tito, and Jawaharlal Nehru, prime minister of India.

At Top Cottage, FDR and his longtime friend and companion Margaret "Daisy" Suckley designed a place for the president to take refuge from the constant barrage of politicians, petitioners, and other visitors who took his open-door policy to an unbearable extreme. Here he worked, read, spent some precious leisure time, and occasionally entertained heads of state including Crown Prince Olav V and Princess Martha of Norway, Winston Churchill, Madame Chiang Kai-shek of China, Crown Princess Louise of Sweden, and Mackenzie King, prime minister of Canada. He also spent time on his back porch admiring more than half a million trees planted on the hillsides and in the valley below, and watching birds among the leaves and branches at the perfect angle for spotting them.

Service to restore the segments of the road on his property, so the original route to Top Cottage remains a rocky, heart-pumping climb to the top of the Roosevelt estate.

Miles and Directions

0.0 Start at the parking lot entrance; turn right and follow the signs for the Hyde Park Trail. Cross the bridge over the brook.

Eleanor's Walk and Top Cottage Trail

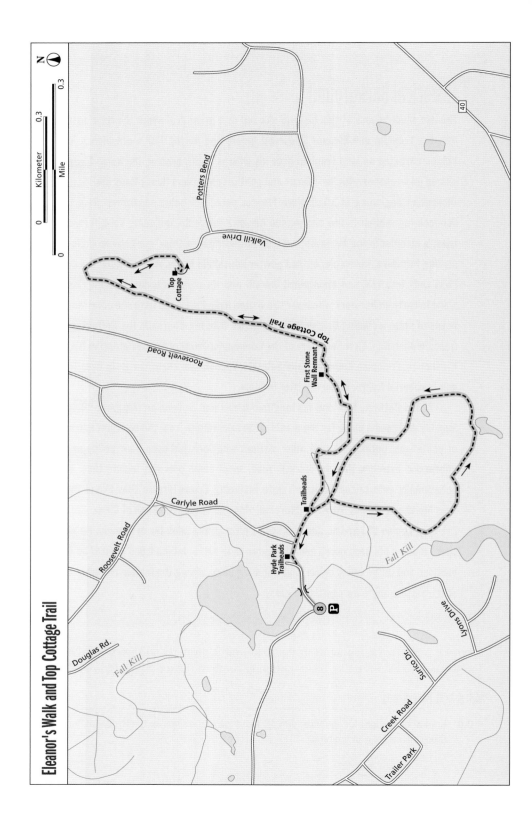

Walk to FDR's private retreat at the height of Top Cottage Trail.

0.1 Turn right from the road onto the Hyde Park Trail. Cross the parking area to the trailhead for Eleanor's Walk/Top Cottage Trail. Follow Eleanor's Walk (red blazes).

0.6 After a steady incline, there's a pond to your right.

1.1 You've completed the Eleanor's Walk loop. Turn right for the Top Cottage Trail (green-and-white Hyde Park Trail markers).

1.4 Cross over the first of several stone wall remnants and start uphill.

2.0 Reach the top of the hill, where the trail ends at a mowed area. Top Cottage is straight ahead. If you collect National Park Passport stamps, there's one here for the Hudson River Valley National Heritage Area. When you've had a chance to visit with the ranger and tour the cottage, head back down the way you came.

2.9 Arrive back at the trailhead. Continue over the bridge to the parking area.

3.1 Arrive back at the parking area.

9 Roosevelt Farm and Forest

Our nation's only four-term president left us this uncommonly lovely woodland, as well as the carriage roads that bring us to its verdant heart.

Start: Roosevelt Farm and Woods Trailhead on NY 9 in Hyde Park, directly across from the Franklin D. Roosevelt Presidential Library
Distance: 2.7-mile loop
Hiking time: About 1.5 hours
Elevation gain: 290 feet
High point: 218 feet
Difficulty: Easy
Best season: Apr through Nov
Traffic: Trail runners, cross-country skiers, cyclists, equestrians

Fees and permits: None to walk the trail; fee to visit the presidential library
Maps: Available at the Henry A. Wallace Visitor Center at Franklin D. Roosevelt Presidential Library and Museum
Trail contact: FDR Presidential Library and Museum, 4079 Albany Post Rd., Hyde Park 12538; (800) FDR-VISIT or (845) 486-7770; fdrlibrary.marist.edu
Special considerations: Take precautions against ticks, mosquitoes, and poison ivy.

Finding the trailhead: From Manhattan take the Henry Hudson Parkway north to the Taconic Parkway; continue to I-84 West. Take I-84 to US 9 North. The FDR Library is on the left side of US 9, 4 miles north of Poughkeepsie; Roosevelt Farm and Woods is on the right side of NY 9, directly across from the library.

From Albany take the New York State Thruway (1-87) south to exit 18 at New Paltz. Take the exit and follow NY 299 East to US 9W South. Cross the Mid-Hudson Bridge and continue to US 9 North. The FDR Library is on the left side of US 9; Roosevelt Farm and Woods is on the right side of NY 9, directly across from the library. GPS: N41 46.194' / W73 55.784'

The Hike

Your walk begins by following the Farm Lane, one of the many carriage roads used by President Franklin Delano Roosevelt and his family and now open only to foot and bicycle traffic. As you near the end of this road, the route we've chosen turns and leads down two woodland trails, immersing you in the kind of forest we read about in storybooks. This mixed forest features many species that are native to the Hudson River Valley: beech, poplar, tulip tree, maple, and oak, as well as eastern hemlock and other conifers. The forest floor's carpet of ferns and many naturally occurring broad-leaf plants is unusually lovely, the result of smart, health-enriching forestry practices still maintained today.

Miles and Directions

0.0   Start at the parking lot. The Farm Lane carriage trail leads east. You'll see trail markers: a white disk with a green tulip-tree leaf. Every 0.1 mile, wooden markers on your left note the distance you've walked.

Historical Background

If you weren't around during the Great Depression or World War II, Franklin Delano Roosevelt's name may be no more to you than one in a list of forty-odd presidents of the United States. For history enthusiasts and those who lived during his four-term presidency, however, the list of Roosevelt's accomplishments extends well beyond the pages of any textbook. One of the least known of these is his devotion to conservation and sustainable farming and forestry, well before the environment became a celebrated cause.

We are fortunate to be able to enjoy the literal fruits of Roosevelt's land preservation efforts here at the last remaining acres of his own farm and forest, saved from development in 2004 by the Scenic Hudson Land Trust and now preserved by the National Park Service. Just across the street, the Home of Franklin D. Roosevelt National Historic Site tells the fascinating story of the president's battle with polio, his life outside the White House, and his relationship with his wife, the venerable First Lady Eleanor Roosevelt. The FDR Presidential Library and Museum fill in all the blanks about the successes that brought this president four terms in the White House: the establishment of Social Security, the New Deal that hastened the end of the Depression, creation of the Civilian Conservation Corps, and his leadership during World War II, to name just a few.

Somewhere in the midst of his twelve-plus years in Washington (Roosevelt died in 1945, just a few months into his fourth term), the president found the time to learn about scientific forestry: the management of a sustainable timber crop with a careful balance between environmental protection and harvesting. At his direction, more than half a million trees were planted on his property here in Hyde Park, creating the strikingly beautiful woodland that surrounds this trail.

0.3 The Red Trail goes left here (it's marked with a wooden sign). Continue straight. In about 30 steps, a path goes right. You will see many of these unmarked paths as you walk down the carriage road.

0.6 The Yellow Trail goes off to the left here. Continue on Farm Lane (bear right at the fork). A stream flows to your left.

0.9 Cross a bridge over a gentle stream. Just after the bridge, a side trail goes left. Continue straight.

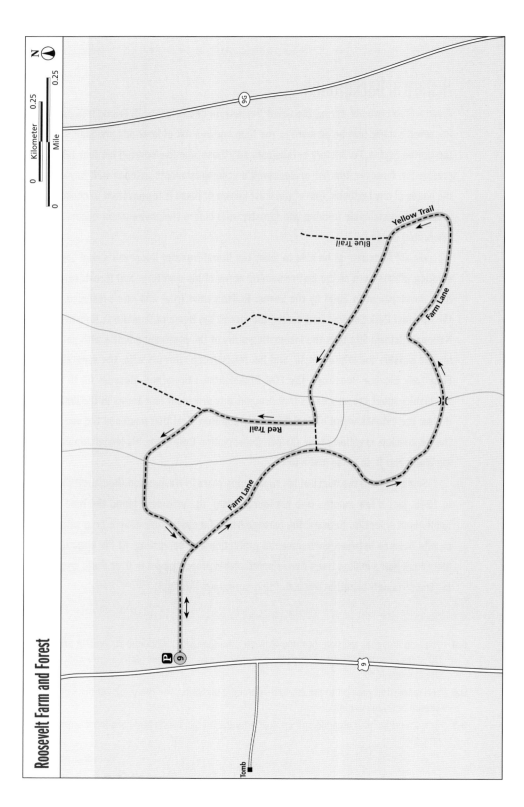

Roosevelt Farm and Forest

Franklin Roosevelt himself enjoyed this trail through his scientifically managed forest.

1.4 The Yellow Trail begins to your left. Turn left onto the Yellow Trail. Follow the yellow blazes on trees, every 20 yards or so.

1.5 The Blue Trail goes right. Continue straight on the Yellow Trail. Note the eastern hemlocks in this section of the woods, lining both sides of the trail.

1.8 At the trail intersection, go left on the Yellow Trail, then left again at the second intersection (just after you cross the stream).

1.9 The Red Trail begins on your right. Turn right and follow the Red Trail. You'll see red blazes on the trees.

2.2 At the trail junction, take the left fork and continue to follow the Red Trail.

2.3 At the junction with three red blazes, turn left.

2.4 Reach the carriage road. Turn right and return to the parking lot.

2.7 Arrive back at the parking lot.

FDR and Scientific Forestry

In his first inaugural address in 1933, Franklin Roosevelt noted his dismay with the waste of American natural resources, especially in the height of the Great Depression, when the nation needed them more than ever. "Nature still offers her bounty and human efforts have multiplied it," he said. "Plenty is at our doorstep, but a generous use of it languishes in the very sight of the supply."

Putting his beliefs into personal practice, Roosevelt applied the principles of scientific forestry to his own property here in the Hudson River Valley. His land in Hyde Park had been farmed for more than 200 years, depleting it of the nutrients required to grow crops. He was certain that turning the land into a tree plantation would rejuvenate it over time, while producing a cash crop of logs for lumber and other construction purposes. Ordering the planting of thousands of tree seedlings every year, Roosevelt filled his fields with healthy native trees, demonstrating their value as a remedy for idle farmland. Over the course of his lifetime, Roosevelt had more than half a million trees planted on his land, creating the expansive forest we come here to explore.

The project not only proved effective but also served as a model for Roosevelt's plans for the entire country. As president, he set programs in motion to restore the over-farmed Dust Bowl lands in Oklahoma by planting trees as windbreaks and as a crop to rejuvenate exhausted soil. His Civilian Conservation Corps planted millions of trees in local, state, regional, and national parks, and agricultural lands across the nation saw renewal as forests took root.

10 Vanderbilt Mansion Loop

See how the other one-millionth percent lived by walking in their footsteps, exploring the lush forests and scenic viewpoints of the very, very rich.

Start: Main parking area for Vanderbilt Mansion National Historic Site
Distance: 2.4-mile loop
Hiking time: About 1.5 hours
Elevation gain: 282 feet
High point: 202 feet
Difficulty: Easy
Best season: Apr through Nov
Traffic: Trail runners, cross-country skiers, cyclists, equestrians, people with dogs

Fees and permits: None to walk the trail; fee to visit the mansion
Maps: Available at the visitor center
Trail contact: Vanderbilt Mansion National Historic Site, 4097 Albany Post Rd., Hyde Park 12538; (845) 229-9115; nps.gov/vama
Special considerations: Take precautions against ticks, mosquitoes, and poison ivy.

Finding the trailhead: From Manhattan take the Henry Hudson Parkway north to the Taconic Parkway; continue to I-84 West. Take I-84 to US 9 North. Vanderbilt Mansion is on the left side of US 9, 4 miles north of Poughkeepsie.

From Albany take the New York State Thruway (1-87) south to exit 18 at New Paltz. Take the exit and follow NY 299 East to US 9W South. Cross the Mid-Hudson Bridge and continue to US 9 North. Vanderbilt Mansion is on the left side of US 9. Park in the lot to the right (north) of the mansion. The trailhead is in the northwest corner of the lot. GPS: N41 48.121' / W73 56.465'

The Hike

If you want to enjoy views of the Hudson River without fighting crowds or dodging trains, and if you would like to see exactly what kinds of benefits staggering amounts of wealth can buy, this hike will give you an ample opportunity to appreciate both. The Vanderbilt Mansion is one of the most popular tourist spots in Hyde Park, but not nearly as many people hike the grounds as fill the house tour. So you can take your time admiring the enormity of the estate, gardens, and grounds and relaxing by the river while others wander through the mansion's opulent rooms.

This walk is part of the Hyde Park Trail, a network of hiking trails neatly linked through a partnership among the Town of Hyde Park, the National Park Service, and other organizations. More than 10 miles in length, the total trail includes Roosevelt Farm and Forest, Home of FDR National Historic Site, Eleanor Roosevelt National Historic Site, Winnakee Nature Preserve, Mills Norrie State Park, and Hackett Hill, Pinewoods, and Riverfront Parks. Find more information about this trail network at hydeparkny.us/Recreation/Trails.

Historical Background

Few names are as closely associated with fabulous nineteenth-century wealth as Cornelius "Commodore" Vanderbilt, the richest man in America in his day. This opulent property belonged to his grandson, Frederick Vanderbilt, who purchased it in 1895. Frederick owned the New York Central Railroad, which passed close to the estate, so he and his family knew that this spot afforded them exceptional views of the Hudson River. The property had fallen into benign neglect when the Vanderbilts acquired it, but Frederick saw the potential in the natural setting and expansive grounds, allowing his love of nature to guide him in selecting a summer home he would share with his wife and children.

The Vanderbilts spent only a few weeks here each summer and winter, but a staff of sixty people maintained the mansion and the 600-acre grounds throughout the year. Frederick himself oversaw the restoration of the gardens and grounds. He ordered the clearing of bridle trails through the woods between the mansion and the river, renovation of the formal Italian gardens, and the construction of a steel-and-concrete bridge over the man-made pond. Today we have Frederick to thank for the peaceful trails, expansive views, and perennial blooms we enjoy on this hike.

Miles and Directions

0.0 Start at the trailhead in the northwest corner of the parking area and begin walking north on the road. The wonderful views of the river begin fairly quickly to your left as you walk.

0.1 The road goes straight and to the right. Continue straight (follow the signs for Bard Rock).

0.2 Leave the road and take the path to your left. Descend on the path and meet up with the road again. (Alternatively, you can skip this shorter path and continue to walk on the road.) Follow the road down to the west, toward the river. The open field to your left is home to goldfinches, meadowlarks, tree swallows, and many other birds.

0.4 A path goes left here. This is the Hyde Park Trail; you'll come back to this shortly. For now, continue straight to see the view from Bard Rock. Cross the one-lane bridge.

0.5 Reach Bard Rock. The view of the river here is unsurpassed. (There's parking here, if you want to return with your vehicle at another time.) When you're ready, turn around and go back across the one-lane bridge to the Hyde Park Trail.

0.6 Turn right on the Hyde Park Trail and begin walking through the woods.

1.2 Vanderbilt Mansion comes into view on the left.

1.3 The trail to the left is a shortcut to the gardens and parking area. Continue straight.

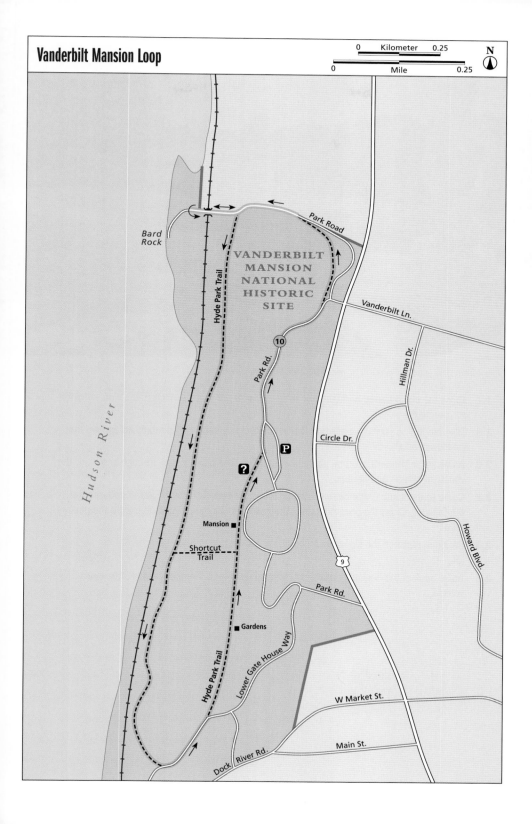

Vanderbilt Mansion Loop

0   Kilometer   0.25
0   Mile   0.25

N

Bard
Rock

Park Road

VANDERBILT
MANSION
NATIONAL
HISTORIC
SITE

Vanderbilt Ln.

Hyde Park Trail

Park Rd.

10

Hillman Dr.

Hudson River

Circle Dr.

P

?

Mansion

Shortcut
Trail

9

Park Rd.

Gardens

Lower Gate House Way

Hyde Park Trail

Howard Blvd.

W Market St.

Main St.

Dock   River Rd.

The Vanderbilt gardens provide a pleasing end to a scenic hike.

1.7 Cross the chain barrier and continue to the road. At the road, turn left (there's an exit gate to your right).

1.8 Take the trail to your left, back into the woods. Begin a short but pronounced ascent. The trail levels off shortly.

2.0 Arrive at the Vanderbilt formal gardens. Take some time here to stroll through and enjoy the variety of shrubs and flowers.

2.2 Come to the south entrance to Vanderbilt Mansion. Bear right on the gravel path around the building. Cross the pavement and continue north on the gravel path toward the parking area.

2.3 Continue north on the sidewalk. At the visitor center, turn right and proceed to the parking lot.

2.4 Arrive back at the beginning of the spacious parking area. Continue across it to your vehicle.

What Happened to the Vanderbilt Fortune?

The $100 million Commodore Vanderbilt amassed in the nineteenth century certainly sounds like it should have been enough to support a family for many generations, but the Vanderbilts that followed had a tough time keeping such a fortune intact. His son William inherited the entire sum and doubled the family's wealth in his lifetime, but when he died, he split the bulk of it between his two sons, Cornelius II and William Kissam Vanderbilt. While Cornelius II continued to manage the New York Central Railroad, William left the business to focus on his Thoroughbred horses and his yachts—two hobbies that did not generate income. The sons built splendid homes in Newport, Rhode Island, including the fabulous mansion known as The Breakers, and they collected old masters and other expensive art, all while increasing their philanthropy—including their naming gift to Vanderbilt University in Nashville. The process of keeping up with the other rich families in their set did nothing to increase the Vanderbilt wealth, and by the time the family's fourth generation inherited the lot, their money quickly went out the door as they worked to keep up appearances. Meanwhile, the New York Central began to lose business as trucks, buses, and airlines ate into its customer base. In 1970 the railroad declared bankruptcy, leaving the Vanderbilts with no income. Today the family's descendants include some fairly high-profile working people: retired fashion designer and novelist Gloria Vanderbilt and her son, CNN journalist Anderson Cooper.

11 Taconic State Park: Copake Falls Mine Area and Bash Bish Falls

Walk from the remains of an 1800s ironworks in New York to a waterfall in Massachusetts.

Start: Main parking area for the Copake Falls developed area in Taconic State Park
Distance: 2.6 miles out and back in two directions
Hiking time: About 1.5 hours
Elevation gain: 392 feet
High point: 1,066 feet
Difficulty: Moderate
Best season: Summer and fall

Traffic: Hikers, joggers, families with children
Fees and permits: Parking fee from Memorial Day to Labor Day
Maps: Available online at nysparks.com/parks/83/maps.aspx
Trail contacts: Taconic State Park, Route 344, Copake Falls 12517; (518) 329-3993; nysparks.com/parks/83/details.aspx

Finding the trailhead: Take I-90 East from Albany to exit B2 for the Taconic State Parkway toward NY 295. Continue 10.7 miles on the parkway to CR 21 and NY 22. Turn left onto CR 21 and drive 5.5 miles to NY 22; bear right. In about 8 miles, turn left onto NY 344 West. Turn right into Taconic State Park, and watch for the parking area on your left. GPS: N42 07.013' / W73 30.472'

The Hike

This hike has two branches in opposite directions, with parking more or less at the midpoint between the two destinations. You may want to do just one of these two hikes during your visit, depending on the amount of time you have available. Both are worthwhile hikes, with the Copake Iron Works a little less traveled than the very popular hike to Bash Bish Falls.

Your hike to the ironworks takes you along the banks of Bash Bish Brook, through an area that was once a center of industrial activity. Interpretive signs along the way help you make sense of the hulking shells of structures left behind when the ironworks shut down in the early 1900s, and an entirely satisfying museum tells the full story about iron as an important commodity to New York's growth and prosperity.

The hike to Bash Bish Falls leads up a well-developed trail and across the state line into Massachusetts. While the history here is perhaps less compelling than the ironworks story, the waterfall itself—split by a rocky outcropping in the middle of the river—is a must-see destination for people traveling through the Taconic Mountains,

Just beyond the Massachusetts border, you can visit Bash Bish Falls. ▶

Historical Background

From its opening in 1845 to its gradual shutdown between 1903 and 1908, Copake Mine Iron Works produced some 4,000 tons of cast iron every year. Oddly enough, even though the mine meant big business in this corner of the Taconic Mountains—with its own railroad stop to transport the iron to industries across the country—very little is known about the business itself. We do know that the ironworks' founder, Lemuel Pomeroy, had worked in the iron trades since he was a young man—giving up college and dreams of becoming an attorney when he discovered an unexpected passion for ironworking. His holding company, Lemuel Pomeroy & Sons of Pittsfield, Massachusetts, ran the Livingston furnace in Ancram for ten years before Pomeroy and his sons discovered the site at Copake Falls. This spot afforded them water power and a strong bed of iron ore, two critical components for a successful operation.

The furnace blasted its first cast iron in 1846, and by 1847 the Copake Iron Company saw the need to add a forge "for the purpose of converting the cast-iron into wrought-iron, and preparing it for use in the manufacture of car-axles and gun-barrels," according to historian Capt. Franklin Ellis in 1878 (usgennet.org/usa/ny/county/columbia/copake/iron_works.htm). Soon roads were built, crews felled acres of trees to turn them into charcoal to keep the furnace running, and the railroad was rerouted to move the iron more efficiently than on the horse-drawn carts the ironworks employed in its early years.

Here you can see the charcoal blast furnace constructed in 1872, the office and brick powder storage building, the brick engine house, a scattering of workers' homes, and one larger home in the Greek Revival style. The Church of St. John in the Wilderness is located here as well.

an area not especially well known to people who do not live nearby. Choose a hiking day in spring or early summer, when the cascade is at its fiercest.

Miles and Directions

0.0 Start in the parking area. You can see trailheads here for Copake Iron Works and Bash Bish Falls. The trail to the ironworks begins west of the parking area; follow the "Trail to Iron Works" sign. Walk through the additional parking area to the bridge, and cross the river.

0.1 Across the bridge on the right, you'll see another "Trail to Iron Works" sign.

Taconic State Park: Copake Falls Mine Area and Bash Bish Falls

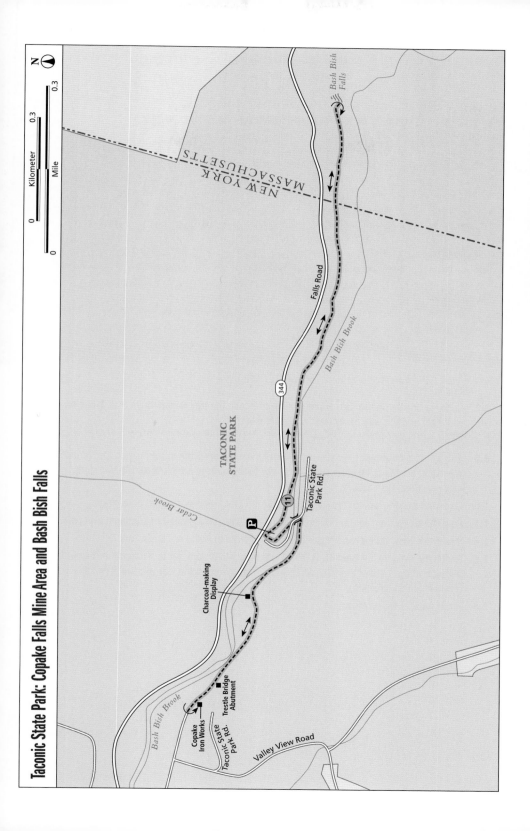

The Copake Falls Iron Works furnace remains at the historic site.

0.2 Come to an interpretive sign about making charcoal. The trail follows Bash Bish Brook on your right and the very pretty Day Pond on the left.

0.4 Reach the trestle bridge abutment.

0.5 Arrive at the ironworks. Here you can explore the forge area, the museum, and the furnace. When you are ready, take the same trail back to the parking area. (***Note:*** The trail signs now say "Bash Bish Falls.")

1.0 Cross the parking area to the Bash Bish Falls Trailhead. Follow the light blue blazes.

1.1 Pass the No Swimming sign. The trail begins to climb; it's a gentle but continuous slope.

1.6 Reach the New York–Massachusetts border. Enter Bash Bish Falls State Park.

1.8 Reach the overlook for Bash Bish Falls. From here, stairs go down to a natural rock viewing platform at the base of the falls. When you are ready, return the way you came (it's all downhill in this direction).

2.6 Arrive back at the parking area.

12 Olana State Historic Site

Walk in the footsteps of some of America's most celebrated artists and see the view that inspired the Hudson River School of painting.

Start: Parking area at the top of the hill, near the Olana mansion
Distance: 1.4-mile loop
Hiking time: About 45 minutes
Elevation gain: 343 feet
High point: 486 feet
Difficulty: Easy
Best seasons: Mar through Nov
Traffic: Joggers, cross-country skiers
Fees and permits: Fee for grounds access on weekends and holidays Apr–Oct. If you prefer not to pay the fee, park in the lot at the base of the hill near the lake and walk up the hill from there.
Maps: Available online at olana.org/visit_tours.php
Trail contact: Olana State Historic Site, 5720 NY 9G, Hudson 12534; (518) 828-0135; olana.org
Special considerations: The admission fee can be credited toward the ticket to tour the house. Reservations are recommended for house tours.

Finding the trailhead: From I-87 North or South, take exit 21 for Catskill. Follow NY 23 east to the Rip Van Winkle Bridge. Cross the bridge and bear right onto NY 9G South. Olana is 1 mile south of the bridge, on the left. Park in the lot at the top of the property, nearest the house. The street address is 5720 NY 9G in Hudson. GPS: N42 13.101' / W73 49.776'

The Hike

An energetic walk through the grounds of this nineteenth-century mansion provides some of the most stunning views of the Hudson River that you can find anywhere along the waterway's length. Each bend in the trail reveals another sweeping landscape with the river in the background, and even the crush of modern development and technology cannot mar the view enough to discourage you from enjoying these expanses. In addition, the path takes you through the well-maintained and carefully selected plantings in Olana's lovely gardens, displaying a variety of native flowers as well as some beautiful and unusual exotic plants.

As if all of this loveliness were not enough to make this a worthwhile hike, your exploration of Olana provides a 343-foot change in elevation, making this an excellent cardio hike as well as one that will make you want to linger. Once you've enjoyed the grounds and seen all the sights, consider a tour of the mansion—one every bit as interesting as its outside might indicate.

Historical Background

Watch the sun sink low over the Hudson River from the grounds of this majestic home, and you will understand how this magnificent view inspired an entirely new style of landscape painting in the mid-nineteenth century. Frederic Edwin Church (1826–1900) lived here in the castle-like mansion at Olana, and his work helped establish the American painting style that came to be known as the Hudson River School.

You may want to go inside and tour the house before taking this walk around the grounds to see some of the paintings Church produced while gazing at the river, the Catskill Mountains, and the Taconic Hills from his studio. Translating these miracles of nature to canvas, Church became one of the most celebrated artists of the Hudson River School, rising to considerable popularity during his lifetime—enough to purchase this property and build the Middle East–inspired home in which he lived with his wife and children.

The viewpoints on these grounds became the backdrop for Church's personal work of art: the 250-acre landscape he designed in an established style known as American picturesque. (Frederick Law Olmsted, the greatest of American landscape designers, created New York's Central Park in this style.) Church established an orchard, planted thousands of trees, installed a lake, and added the carriage trails that we can walk today. Closer to the house, you can see a cutting garden created for Mrs. Church to provide cut flowers for the house.

This hike provides the complete picture—expansive views, stretches of dense forest, and opportunities to stop and smell the flowers that grace the hillside closest to the Persian-style mansion.

Miles and Directions

0.0 Start from the parking area and take the brick stairway down to the carriage road. At the bottom, cross the road and begin walking on the carriage road.

0.1 Stop here to view the house from the outside. Bear left at the fork. The mansion is on your right as the formal garden comes into view. Depending on the season, you may see peony, iris, black-eyed Susan, purple salvia, honeysuckle, allium, and many other plants in

The mansion at Olana is the unique vision of artist Frederic Edwin Church.

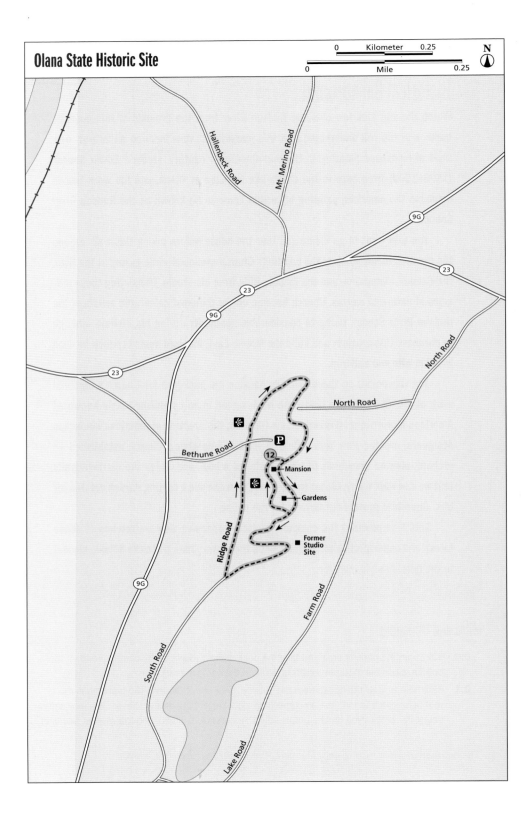

Olana State Historic Site

0   Kilometer   0.25

0   Mile   0.25

N

Hallenbeck Road

Mt. Merino Road

9G

23

9G

23

23

North Road

North Road

9G

P

12

Bethune Road

Mansion

Gardens

Ridge Road

Former
Studio
Site

Farm Road

South Road

Lake Road

bloom. After the garden, the trail continues through an open meadow. Your first view of the Hudson River is directly in front of you.

0.3 As you come to the farthest bend in the carriage road, the Hudson Valley landscape opens in front of you. Even the three radio towers do not mar the extraordinary view. The carriage road turns left here.

0.4 Reach the site of Church's former studio (which no longer stands). Not surprisingly, it features one of the finest views of the river and valley you've seen so far. Art historians call this "one of the most celebrated [views] in American art and landscape history." From here, continue to the road and turn right, walking along the road for a short stretch.

0.6 Turn right on the carriage road marked "Ridge Road." Shortly come to a path to the left; this is the route down to the main road used by the Churches and their guests. Pass this intersection and continue straight, bearing right at this fork.

0.7 Come to an open area on the right. It has a marshy bottom, so you may see a significant difference in the vegetation here. This is one of the best places to view the mansion's towers.

0.8 Your walk up this gentle but steady incline is rewarded with the Hudson River view you came to Olana to see. As you walk the next level stretch, the Rip Van Winkle Bridge comes into view. Continue on the carriage road.

1.1 You can turn right here to return to the house and the parking area. If you want to go down to the lake, continue straight (bear left at fork) onto North Road. At the junction, continue around to the visitor center and house. The view from behind the house is one of the best on the property. As you walk from the house, you'll pass above the cultivated garden you saw earlier. You may want to stop here and stroll through the garden to enjoy the plantings.

1.2 Turn left to complete the loop.

1.4 Arrive back at the parking area.

13 Kingston Point Rotary Park

This neighborhood park plays host to one of the Hudson River's lighthouses, making it an essential stop on any tour of the river's maritime history.

Start: Park entrance on Delaware Avenue in Kingston
Distance: 1.4 miles out and back
Hiking time: About 1 hour
Elevation gain: 29 feet, mostly below sea level
High point: 7 feet
Difficulty: Easy

Best season: Spring through fall
Traffic: Hikers, joggers, cyclists
Fees and permits: No fees or permits required
Map: Available online at kingston-ny.gov/content/8401/10588/10622/default.aspx
Trail contacts: The Rotary Club of Kingston, PO Box 3581, Kingston 12402; kingstonrotary.org

Finding the trailhead: From Broadway in Kingston, take Delaware Avenue to its terminus at Kingston Point. Watch for the metal gates to the park at the end of Delaware Avenue. Park at the end of Delaware, and walk toward the river to reach the gates. GPS: N41 55.699' / W73 57.905'

The Hike

Hidden away behind a gate at the end of a residential street, Kingston Point Rotary Park remains the well-kept secret of this Westchester County community, a spot that

Your hike follows the railroad tracks that once brought thousands of visitors a day to Kingston Point.

Historical Background

Back in the late 1890s, Cornell Steamboat Company and Ulster & Delaware Railroad president Samuel Decker Coykendall saw a tremendous opportunity to increase his already substantial income—by making Kingston Point a destination for travelers heading up and down the Hudson River. He filled in an area of marshy wetland here and built a dance hall, the Oriental Hotel, pavilions, a gazebo, bridges, picturesque lagoons, and arcades, adding a carousel and other amusements for children to make Kingston Point a family outing. At the same time, the clever Coykendall extended the tracks of the U&D Railroad to the point and arranged for the Cornell Steamboat Company's Day Line to stop here on its way up and down the river. Travelers could disembark from the steamboat and get right on a train to take them to the Catskills.

With so much access and so many opportunities for fun, Kingston Point became one of the hot spots of the Hudson River Valley from the late 1800s to 1922. Just as the twenties began to roar, however, fire struck the Oriental Hotel and the structure burned to the ground. This signaled the beginning of the end for the amusement park and attractions, and by the time the Great Depression arrived in 1929, the entire park had fallen into disrepair.

Kingston Point stood decaying from within and without until the 1990s, when the Rotary Club of Kingston made the point its civic project. Seeing the historical significance as well as the natural beauty of this park, the Rotary preserved some of the amusement park's interesting structures while creating pathways, cleaning up meadows and woodlands, and clearing the way for visitors to enjoy spectacular views of the river and its charms. Today the city of Kingston honors the Rotary's heroic work by calling the site Kingston Point Rotary Park; your own visit here underscores the success of the Rotary's reclamation effort.

The Hudson River Maritime Museum has a hand in Kingston Point as well, as the caretakers of Rondout Lighthouse. The light stands at the mouth of Rondout Creek— just as it has since 1915—and its light still shines every night to help ship captains navigate the river. You can learn more about the light's importance to the river and the region by visiting the maritime museum at 50 Rondout Landing, in Kingston's bustling historic district.

most visitors are not likely to discover on their own. It not only provides the only viewpoint for Rondout Creek Lighthouse on the west side of the Hudson River but also delights visitors with its level trail and its panoramic views of the river. Your walk follows the Ulster & Delaware Railroad tracks that once brought thousands of people to Kingston Point's amusement park, a center of diversionary activity during the Victorian era. Here too are the remains of the boat wharf at which the Hudson River Day Line docked, unloading passengers from as far south as New York City and as far north as Albany.

While the hike here is not long, you're bound to want to linger and enjoy this particularly attractive part of the river. The path ends fairly suddenly at a gravel drive that leads out to North Street. We took this route to try to create a loop trail, and found the walk along the road against traffic to be more harrowing than most walkers prefer. Instead, walk back the way you came and take the opportunity to see the river from the opposite direction.

Kingston Point is the best place to see the Rondout Lighthouse.

Kingston Point Rotary Park

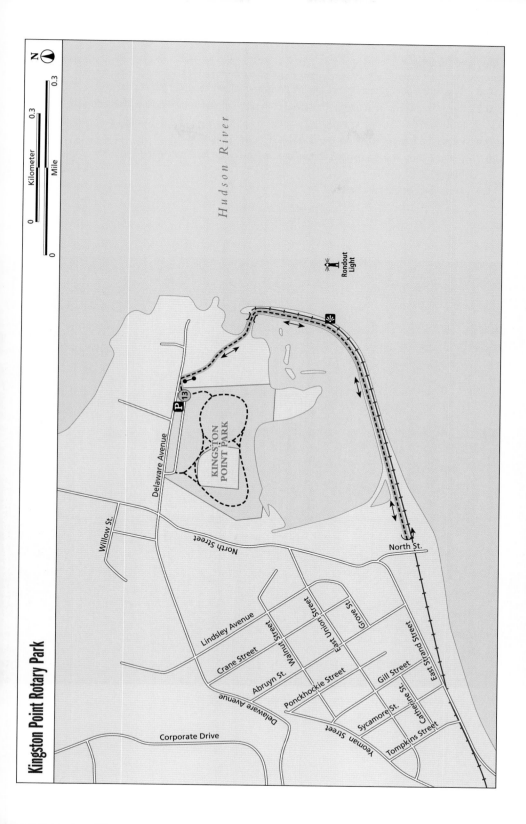

Hudson River

Rondout Light

KINGSTON POINT PARK

P 13

Delaware Avenue

Willow St.

North Street

North St.

Lindsley Avenue

Crane Street

Abruyn St.

Walnut Street

East Union Street

Grove St.

Ponckhockie Street

Gill Street

Sycamore St.

Catherine St.

East Strand Street

Yeoman Street

Tompkins Street

Delaware Avenue

Corporate Drive

N

Kilometer
0   0.3

Mile
0   0.3

Miles and Directions

0.0   Start at the park gates. Go through the gates and follow the gravel path to the river.

0.2   Cross a waterway on a bridge. The gravel path runs parallel to the Hudson River and to a railroad track.

0.3   Reach the best viewpoint for the Rondout (Kingston) Lighthouse.

0.7   The trail ends at a gravel drive. Return the way you came for a different perspective on the Hudson River view.

1.4   Arrive back at the park gates.

Reeds and cattails form a boundary between hikers and rivers.

Capital District

Views of the Hudson River are just one of the many features of the Wilkinson National Recreation Trail.

14 John Boyd Thacher State Park: Indian Ladder Trail

Limestone cliffs, spectacular valley views, hanging gardens, jagged rock formations, and coves behind waterfalls: This is the must-see trail in the Capital region.

Start: The Indian Ladder Trailhead is at the west end of the parking area—take the connecting road to the additional parking, and drive as far as you can.
Distance: 1.6-mile lollipop
Hiking time: About 1 hour
Elevation gain: 317 feet
High point: 1,180 feet
Difficulty: Easy
Best season: May through Oct
Traffic: Hikers only
Fees and permits: Fee per vehicle on weekends and holidays; none all other days

Maps: Available online at parks.ny.gov/parks/128/maps.aspx
Trail contact: John Boyd Thacher State Park, 1 Hailes Cave Rd., Voorheesville 12186; (518) 872-9133; parks.ny.gov/parks/128/details.aspx
Special considerations: Some steep drop-offs and views from high places; not recommended for very young children. This hike features 110 stairs going down at its outset and 110 going up at the end of the gorge hike.

Finding the trailhead: From Voorheesville take NY 85A (Helderberg Parkway / New Salem Road) west and south to the junction with NY 85 (New Scotland Road). Turn right onto NY 85 and continue to the junction with NY 157. Turn right onto NY 157 and continue to the park. Park in the last lot at the end of the bank of parking areas. The trail begins at GPS: N42 39.106' / W74 00.426'

The Hike

Towering limestone walls, waterfalls originating above and below the trail, and overhangs that allow us to stand behind tumbling waters are just a few of the delights this trail produces. Remember to look behind you to catch the hanging gardens that spring forth when water seeps through porous rock walls, and to peer deep into holes in the rock to glimpse the origins of trickling streams. Don't be surprised if a chipmunk comes up to your shoe and waits expectantly—wildlife here seems to know that people mean food, but feeding the chipmunks or any other animals is illegal. Try not to be taken in by a striped, 4-inch-high bandit.

You can walk the Indian Ladder Trail to its end, turn around, and walk back on the same trail or climb the 110 steps at the far end and return on the level trail at the rim of the cliff. The rim trail delivers panoramic valley views and provides an easy return route if you've had enough of stairs, rocks, and ledges.

The Indian Ladder Trail features a horsetail waterfall, shallow caves, and other fascinating natural features. ▶

Historical Background

Of the many excellent hiking opportunities in the greater Albany area, Indian Ladder Trail stands out as the best representation of central New York's geological story. The hike traces an edge of the Helderberg Escarpment, where the collision of continents hundreds of millions of years ago forced limestone, sandstone, and shale peaks up from the depths of Earth's bedrock. Over eons, wind and weather wore away the sharp peaks and left behind this long range of cliffs, breaking away great limestone slabs and leaving a rock wall perpendicular to the valley floor at its base.

Fast-forward to about a thousand years ago, when the Schoharie Indians came through here regularly on a path along the rock ridgeline we see today. Descending from the cliff above on makeshift ladders, the Indians followed the path behind waterfalls and over tricky rock faces, then climbed a ladder at the other end and returned to higher ground. Today we call this the Indian Ladder Trail, but the ladders are gone—although they were in use as recently as the 1950s—and we now climb down sturdy metal staircases to gain access to the visual riches below.

Miles and Directions

0.0 Start from the parking area. Before you begin your hike, enjoy the view of the valley below. To your right you can see the very tall building standing parallel to four identical smaller buildings: These are all part of Empire State Plaza, the center of the Capital District in downtown Albany. The trail begins at the stone staircase to your left. Follow the aqua blazes.

0.2 Emerge from the trail along the rim in a mowed picnic area. Continue along the edge on the trail, which gives you another chance to admire the view.

0.4 At the end of the picnic area, take the stairs down. There are 110 steps in all, some metal and some stone. You'll come to a part of the staircase with a low ceiling—a natural overhang that's about 4.5 feet high. Stoop to go through it, and come out on the Talus Slope, a particularly striking area of rock formations. Go down another eleven steps into an area where water drips down the rock wall, creating hanging gardens of ferns and mosses.

0.5 You're behind Minelot Falls, under an overhang that extends the falls out in front of you. Note that there's water coming down behind you as well, pouring over the rock wall. The water wore holes in the rock over many years. It's easy to spot the wet areas, because plant life grows here wherever there's running water. From here, cross a short boardwalk and go down eleven steps toward the second falls.

John Boyd Thacher State Park: Indian Ladder Trail

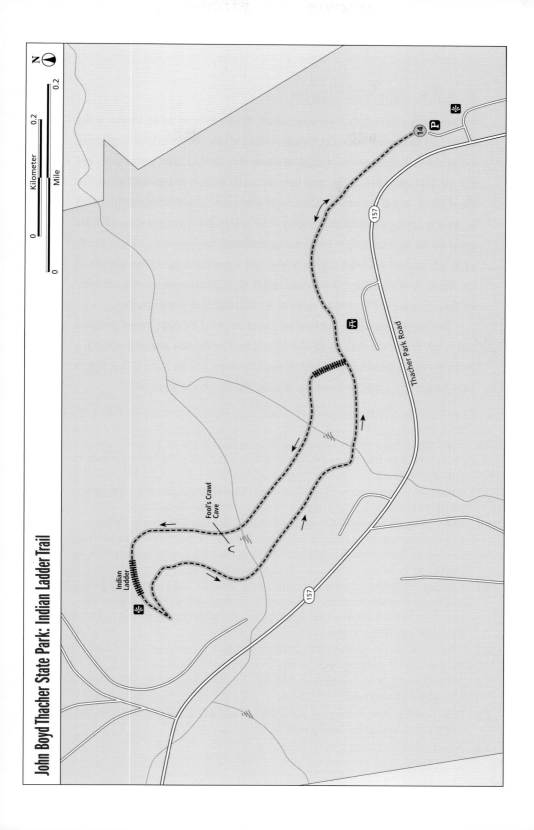

Who Was John Boyd Thacher?

His name was a household word during nearly two decades of public service to the Albany area and beyond, but today, John Boyd Thacher's life and works have largely been lost to history. Thacher served as mayor of Albany from 1886 to 1888, and again for two years in 1896 and 1897. At the same time, he and his brother George ran Thacher Car Wheel Works, one of the leading industries in Albany, and John devoted a great deal of his time to writing publications on topics of US history. His books and papers include works on the nomenclature of the American continent, the exploration of John Cabot, a two-volume work on Christopher Columbus, and a remarkable book titled *Outlines of the French Revolution Told in Autographs*, which highlights his own collection of autographs—including one from every signer of the Declaration of Independence.

This might be enough to put Thacher's name on one of the state's most gorgeous parks, but the fact is that he purchased this land in the late nineteenth century. Thacher's wife, Emma Treadwell Thacher, donated this land to the state of New York in 1914 for use as a public park, and the state named the park in his honor.

0.6 Reach the second waterfall—actually two falls, one cascading from above and one falling just in front of you. Watch your step here; the stream that feeds this waterfall crosses the stone path here.

0.7 Come to an alcove where you'll find Fool's Crawl Cave, on the course of an underground stream. Look down the rocks to see this stream tumble down the cliff face.

0.8 Reach a huge natural archway that's worth exploration—there are openings for shallow caves at either side. Then continue to the staircase at the end of the path. It's sixty-two stairs up to a scenic landing and then twelve steps down from the landing to a viewing platform.

0.9 A viewing deck offers a fairly unobstructed view of the valley below—a strikingly green sight in spring and summer. When you're ready, return up these twelve steps and go up forty-eight more to return to the cliff rim. Turn left and walk back along the rim trail (still blazed aqua) and into the picnic area.

1.1 Cross this stream on stepped rocks straight ahead, or go around to your right about 100 feet and take the bridge across.

1.2 Join the paved path and continue on the bridge over the stream. The second waterfall you saw below originates here.

1.3 Steps here lead down to the path you followed on your way in, along the rim of the cliff. Take this path back to the parking area.

1.6 Arrive back at the parking area.

15 Peebles Island State Park

Where the Mohawk and Hudson Rivers meet, the shirt and collar industry once dominated the US textile market.

Start: North end of the parking lot, past the Bleachery complex
Distance: 2.0-mile loop
Hiking time: About 1 hour
Elevation gain: 108 feet
High point: 48 feet
Difficulty: Easy
Best season: Apr through Oct
Traffic: Trail runners, cross-country skiers

Fees and permits: Fee per vehicle on weekends and holidays May through Oct; none all other times
Maps: Available at the park visitor center (open Wed–Sun) or online at nysparks.com/parks/attachments/PeeblesIslandTrailMap.pdf
Trail contact: Peebles Island State Park, PO Box 295, Waterford 12188; (518) 237-7000; nysparks.com/parks/111/details.aspx
Special considerations: Take precautions against ticks, mosquitoes, and poison ivy.

Finding the trailhead: From I-90, take exit 6A (I-787 North) to Cohoes. Continue on I-787 as it becomes NY 787. At the fourth traffic light, turn right onto Ontario Street (NY 470). Just before the Hudson River bridge to Troy, turn left onto Delaware Avenue. The bridge to Peebles Island is at the end of Delaware Avenue. Park at the north end of the parking lot, past the Bleachery complex. The trail begins on a crushed gravel path. GPS: N42 47.098' / W73 40.852'

The Hike

Steeped in industrial history but most popular for its terrific views of the Mohawk and Hudson Rivers, Peebles Island is a favorite hiking ground for residents of Troy and the smaller towns north of Albany. It's no wonder that this place draws visitors at any time of day and in every season. A wilderness on the edge of a formerly major manufacturing district, the island offers 191 acres of respite from the largely commercialized areas that surround it.

The dense woods lead you to high bluffs over the Mohawk River, where the town of Waterford is visible just across the water. As the path continues, a series of islands come into view: Bock, Goat, Polderump, and Second Islands appear on the west side of Peebles Island, along with one of the many dams built to prevent major flooding in central New York's numerous wet seasons.

At the south end of the island, you can view the split the island forms in the river; soon rocky shoals appear as you walk north on the island's east side. The uneven, sedimentary rock–strewn riverbed creates a stretch of rushing whitewater here in late winter and spring.

Historical Background

You won't be able to miss the former Cluett, Peabody & Company Powerhouse as you enter the park. Now serving as the park's visitor center, as well as the headquarters for the Erie Canalway National Heritage Corridor, this turn-of-the-twentieth-century edifice housed the Bleachery complex for the company that supplied manufacturing services to Arrow Shirt Company. Cluett, Peabody & Company was the principal maker of the famous Arrow collars—detachable shirt collars that became a wardrobe staple for the common man in the 1910s and 1920s. Brilliant advertising turned Cluett, Peabody into the most successful company in the United States in the 1920s, turning out 4 million collars a week. The company continued to function here until 1972. You can learn more by visiting the building and seeing the extensive interpretive displays in the visitor center.

In addition to the industrial story, Peebles Island tells an Erie Canal story as well. A pedestrian bridge here takes you to Canal Lock #2, just across the Mohawk River in Waterford. This lock has been enlarged and modernized since the canal's original construction in the 1820s, but it remains as one of only thirty-five of the original eighty-three locks that raised and lowered barges and ships along the length of the canal from Albany to Buffalo. Here the canal is at one of its lower points. The canal rises 566 feet from the Hudson River to Lake Erie, with its lowest point near here in Troy.

Miles and Directions

0.0 Start from the parking area and walk west on the crushed-gravel path. Watch along the trail for groundhogs living in the generous understory as you approach the woods, and for deer in just about any area along the trail.

0.2 Bear right at the fork in the trail and enter Oak Grove. Continue to bear right as the trail splinters twice more.

0.3 A side path goes to the right. Take this path to reach a great view of the river; it will rejoin the main path shortly.

0.5 This point on the island provides the first wide-open view of the water. Soon this side trail rejoins the main trail. Continue straight. You can see the town of Waterford across the river, and Bock Island is coming into view on the left.

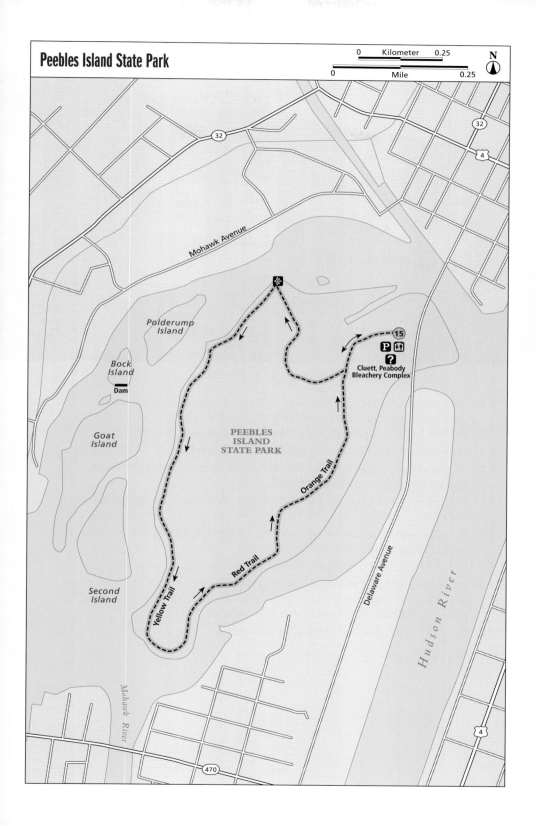

Peebles Island State Park

0   Kilometer   0.25

0   Mile   0.25

N

Mohawk Avenue

Polderump
Island

Bock
Island

Dam

Goat
Island

PEEBLES
ISLAND
STATE PARK

Orange Trail

Red Trail

Yellow Trail

Second
Island

Cluett, Peabody
Bleachery Complex

Delaware Avenue

Hudson River

Mohawk River

The Bleachery building once housed part of the Arrow collar manufacturing operation.

0.6 A trail marked with red-plastic disks goes left. There's a little pavilion here. Continue straight, and bear right ahead for another terrific view of the river. The dam is to the right, and Bock Island is now straight ahead. Goat Island is past the dam to the right.

0.7 You're now parallel to the dam. Second Island is coming into view.

1.2 Continue straight, now on the yellow-marked trail. (The red trail goes left.) You're now rounding the southernmost part of the island.

1.3 A rocky area in the river creates a short falling-water phenomenon, with accompanying rapids.

1.4 The yellow-marked trail goes left here, while the red goes right. Take the red-marked trail to the right to stay on the island's perimeter.

1.7 Turn right on the mowed-grass path. (The red trail continues left.) Enter the woods.

1.8 Turn left onto the orange-marked trail. Shortly emerge in a meadow that sports tall grasses and leafy plants in summer. Continue straight as you reach the paved area, and cross behind the Bleachery complex to return to the parking lot.

2.0 Complete the loop and arrived back at the parking area.

16 Saratoga National Historical Park: Wilkinson National Recreation Trail

Rolling fields, robust forests, and a dash of history—this hike tours the Revolutionary War battlefield in Saratoga while passing wildflower-rich meadows and bushes laden with berries.

Start: Go out the back door of the Saratoga National Historical Park visitor center to reach the Wilkinson trailhead.
Distance: 4.2-mile lollipop
Hiking time: About 2.25 hours
Elevation gain: 391 feet
High point: 447 feet
Difficulty: Moderate
Best seasons: Apr–Oct
Traffic: Trail runners, cross-country skiers; perhaps equestrians on connecting trails
Fees and permits: Fee per hiker May 1–Oct 31, valid for seven days. The annual National

Federal Recreation Lands Pass covers this fee; an annual pass just for this park is also available.
Maps: Available at the park visitor center or online at nps.gov/sara/planyourvisit
Trail contact: Saratoga National Historical Park, 648 Rte. 32, Stillwater 12170; (518) 664-9821; nps.gov/sara
Special considerations: Pick up an interpretive trail brochure at the visitor center, and follow the battle's progress as you arrive at each tour stop. Take precautions against ticks and mosquitoes.

Finding the trailhead: From Albany take I-87 (Northway) to exit 12. Turn right off the exit ramp onto NY 67 East, and stay to the right as you go through the traffic circle. After the circle, bear left as you enter the next traffic circle, and take the exit for US 9 North (on your right). Continue 1.6 miles to the second traffic light, and turn right (east) onto NY 9P. Drive 4.5 miles along Saratoga Lake, and turn right (east) onto NY 423. Continue 5.5 miles to NY 32, and turn right (east) into Saratoga National Historical Park. Park in the main lot, located below the visitor center. The trail begins at the back door of the visitor center. GPS: N43 00.723' / W73 38.932'

The Hike

The Wilkinson National Recreation Trail explores the northern section of Saratoga National Historical Park, linking in several places with the park's driving tour road and its interpretive displays. The former fields of the McBride and Freeman farms, which gave up their harvest in 1777 to soldiers on both sides of the Revolutionary War, are now overseen by the National Park Service and are similar to the way they appeared during the eighteenth century.

If you feel you learned all you needed to know about the Revolutionary War in high school, you'll still find plenty to enjoy on this trail—opportunities for bird and butterfly identification abound, and many native wildflower varieties bloom here throughout spring and summer. In fall, when the fields turn gold and violet as they

Historical Background

On this ground in the fall of 1777, two battles pitted the well-organized, highly trained British Regulars against a fiercely determined and much larger army of the newly created United States of America, and signaled a sea change in the war for American independence. What the British considered a shallow rebellion turned into a conflict involving countries from the reaches of eastern and western Europe. And while fighting continued for another six years, the Americans gained an advantage at Saratoga that would eventually result in a new nation conceived in liberty.

In late summer, Gen. John Burgoyne led the British Regulars south from Canada in what seemed like an advantageous invasion, using a corridor of waterways including Lake Champlain to penetrate the new American state of New York. The British expected to meet another of their armies coming east through Lake Ontario and the Mohawk River, but American Gen. Horatio Gates and his army blocked the British troops at Albany, foiling their planned meeting and leaving Burgoyne and his men on their own. Daunted but not discouraged, Burgoyne continued his approach to the American forces at Saratoga.

Meanwhile, the Americans built fortifications here on the soon-to-be battlefield at Bemis Heights, according to specifications supplied by Polish engineer Thaddeus Kosciusko, a brilliant strategist who pledged loyalty to the American forces throughout the war. Bemis Heights provided dense woodlands, ravines, and swamplands just below the fortifications, restricting Burgoyne's mobility should he choose to advance. The placement of the American fort forced Burgoyne to move inland, away from the Hudson River. The trail you will follow here at Saratoga traces the road Burgoyne used on his way to battle.

Burgoyne split his men into three columns: one that took the road along the Hudson, one that marched a mile farther west of the river, and the last one marching a mile even farther inland. With no hope of reinforcements coming to relieve his men and no supplies coming up the river to his position, however, his strategy could not compete against the many hardships his troops endured. Heat, cold, rain, blackflies and mosquitoes, and hunger as rations ran out all plagued the British soldiers as they readied to take on the Americans.

On September 19, 1777, the British finally advanced south. Riflemen led by American officer Daniel Morgan rushed forward to meet them, and the two armies engaged in three hours of heated fighting. Just as it looked as though the British would fall, a contingent of German artillery arrived with two cannons, firing into the American lines and scattering the troops. The Americans had no choice but to withdraw, and the British celebrated a victory—but their success came at the cost of hundreds of lives. With no other reinforcements on their way, the British faced a harsh reality: The American forces grew with each passing day as volunteers and organized troops arrived to fortify their ranks, while they blocked all the routes that Loyalist forces might take to bring Burgoyne the food, supplies, and men he needed to secure a victory.

Over the next several weeks, Burgoyne's men built defensive redoubts, clearing the trees from several acres of land to strengthen their fort walls and remove obstructions in front of lookout points. On October 7, the general finally decided it was time to make a move, before his depleted ranks succumbed to the coming winter cold. He and 1,500 men marched into Simeon Barber's farm field, and Horatio Gates gave the order to advance against the British. The armies fought their way toward Balcarres Redoubt at Freeman's farm, until the Americans captured Breymann Redoubt and Burgoyne saw that he had no choice but to retreat. The British left Saratoga as darkness fell on the battlefield and headed north toward Schuylerville with 1,200 fewer men in their ranks than when they arrived three weeks earlier.

Lt. William Wilkinson, a British officer, mapped this route during the battle as his troops and others marched through these fields and over the hills. Thanks to his efforts, we can now truly walk in the footsteps of the opposition forces and see the landscape much as they saw it, from their ascent out of the Great Ravine to their defensive positions in the congested woods. Interpretive signs along the way give you details about the battle, defensive and offensive positions, military strategy, and the innovations on the American side that led to the defeat of the British Regulars. You also can enjoy an audio tour on your cell phone—just call the number you will see on signs at each tour stop.

The now-peaceful Saratoga battlefield belies the pivotal confrontation that took place here centuries ago.

fill with goldenrod and New York and New England asters, the hardwood forests offer multihued landscapes of scarlet, topaz, and aubergine as their leaves succumb to autumn. It's a great time to be out-of-doors, and this trail is one of the best in New York for enjoying both natural sights and a pivotal moment in American history.

Miles and Directions

0.0 Start at the visitor center, where you'll pay the admission fee. Walk out the back door of the center and follow the footpath to the kiosk that signals the trailhead.

0.3 Bear left (east) on the grassy trail at Station A. Follow the brown signs that say "Wilkinson Trail" in white print. In spring and summer look for sensitive fern, black-eyed Susan, goldenrod, joe-pye weed, common yarrow, and several species of milkweed (including the striking orange butterfly weed) in the meadow.

0.5 The trail crosses the park's "H" (Horse) trail. Continue straight.

0.6 A side trail leads to interpretive material about Breymann Redoubt, a British fortification built by Loyalist, German, and Canadian troops. The stop is optional but recommended for its interesting historical content. When you're ready, return to the Wilkinson Trail and continue to the left (south).

0.8 Bear left (southeast) as the loop begins at the tour's Station C.

1.1 Cross the tour road and enter a mixed wood of pine and scrub oak. There are lots of berry bushes here and in many places along the trail; look for blackberries and black raspberries, which ripen in late July. Berry eating is permitted in the park.

Saratoga National Historical Park: Wilkinson National Recreation Trail

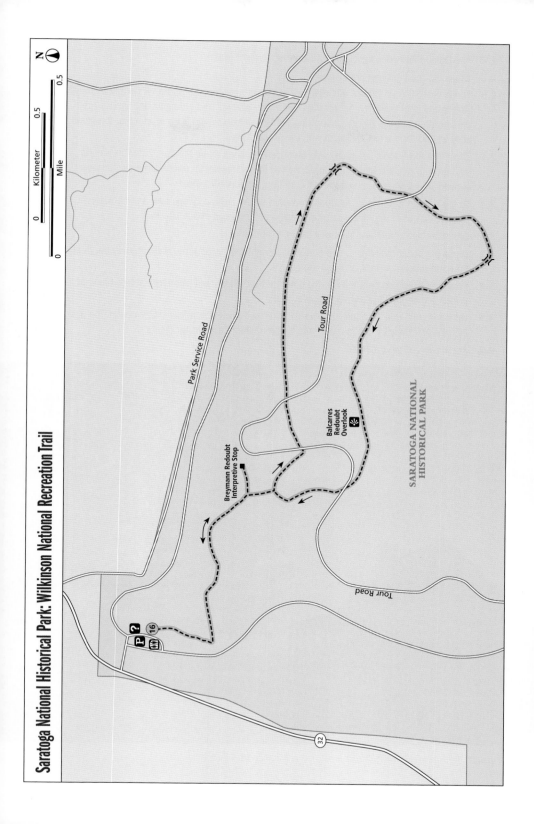

1.2 The Liaison Trail goes right (south). Continue straight (east).

1.3 Cross the road and continue straight.

1.9 Cross the "ST" trail. There's a bridge over a stream as you reach Station F. Continue straight and to the right (south), and enter an open field of ferns and emerging aspen. This area was farmland during the war, supplying the British troops with fresh produce to forage as they waited for the next skirmish with the Americans.

2.1 Cross the road. You'll see many wild blackberry bushes along the trail. Enter the woods and cross a ditch in which the British waited for two weeks for reinforcements that never arrived. In a few steps, begin the descent into the Great Ravine.

2.4 At the bottom of the long, gradual downward slope, cross a bridge over a stream. Begin the ascent out of the ravine—a total elevation increase of about 120 feet.

3.1 Cross the paved trail and continue straight (northwest).

3.2 Cross the paved trail again, and continue straight (northwest). You're heading in the direction of the visitor center, as signs indicate.

3.3 Cross the road and bear left (north) onto the trail. Watch and listen for eastern bluebirds, bobolinks, and field sparrows in these fields.

3.5 Complete the loop. Turn left (northwest) and head back toward the visitor center. The trail inclines gradually for the last 0.7 mile to the trailhead and visitor center.

4.2 Arrive back at the trailhead.

Farmers John and Lydia Neilson built this red house in 1775 or 1776.

Adirondack Region

The new trail leads to the best possible view of OK Slip Falls.

17 Hooper Garnet Mine

Bring your rock hammer and make the most of this abandoned mine, where gemstones sparkle on the surfaces of ancient rock.

Start: Parking area at the Garnet Hill Lodge, 30 Garnet Hill Rd. Section 2, in North River
Distance: 1.4 miles out and back
Hiking time: About 1 hour
Elevation gain: 184 feet
High point: 2,137 feet
Difficulty: Moderate
Best season: Summer and fall
Traffic: Hikers only
Fees and permits: No fees or permits required
Maps: Available online at garnet-hill.com/wp-content/pdf/SkiTrailMap.pdf

Trail contacts: Garnet Hill Lodge, 30 Garnet Hill Rd. Section 2, North River 12856; (518) 251-2444; garnet-hill.com
Special considerations: You need to ask permission to park at Garnet Hill Lodge if you are not a guest of the resort. Stop at the lodge (or at the ski shop, if you choose to park there and skip the hike from the lodge) to check with a staff member about leaving your car while you hike.

Finding the trailhead: From NY 28 in North River, turn southwest onto CR 78 (13th Lake Road). Stay on CR 78 / 13th Lake Road as it winds through the North River area. At the intersection with 4-H Road and Garnet Hill Road Section 2, turn left onto Garnet Hill Road Section 2. This road ends at Garnet Hill Lodge, where you'll park. GPS: N43 42.735' / W74 06.399'

The Hike

A fairly rugged hike along cross-country ski trails to a rocky incline, this trek to the Hooper Garnet Mine rewards in unusual ways. There's the tangible reward of collecting actual garnets, a red gemstone, and bringing back these sparkly stones as souvenirs of your efforts. Beyond the gems, this spot offers one of the best views of the High Peaks region for the least actual effort.

You will pay for these benefits, however, as you walk up the boulder-strewn slope to get to the former mine. Boots with ankle support are a necessity for this trail, as the trail itself serves as a route for spring runoff from the mountains—bringing all the loose rocks down the hill every year and leaving them scattered throughout the trail. It's barely 0.3 mile from the base of this slope to the mine, but you will feel as though you had a good workout by the time you reach the top.

Miles and Directions

0.0 Start at the lodge and take the trail to the ski shop. At the intersection with the trail to the ski shop and Porcupine Pass, take the trail with the sign that says "Easier Way to the Ski Shop."

Historical Background

Not many of today's New Yorkers know that the Adirondacks were once one of the world's leading producers of garnets, the red gemstones removed from the rock using brute force and some clever sluicing techniques. Industries that use abrasives prized Adirondack garnets above all others because of the way these gems fracture, providing just the right amount of roughness for sandpaper and rubbing compounds used in manufacturing.

Here in the shadow of Balm of Gilead Mountain, Frank Hooper started an open-pit mine in 1898 to rival the already successful Barton Mine on the other side of Gore Mountain. Hooper came up with an ingenious process that used water to separate the garnet from the rock, employing a system of pipes and the properties of the garnet to separate the gems from the tailings. The Hooper Mine never achieved the success of the Barton Mine, but the garnets are still here in the rock, waiting for ambitious hikers with rock hammers to tap them out.

Bring your rock hammer to take home some garnets in your visit to Hooper Mine.

Hooper Garnet Mine

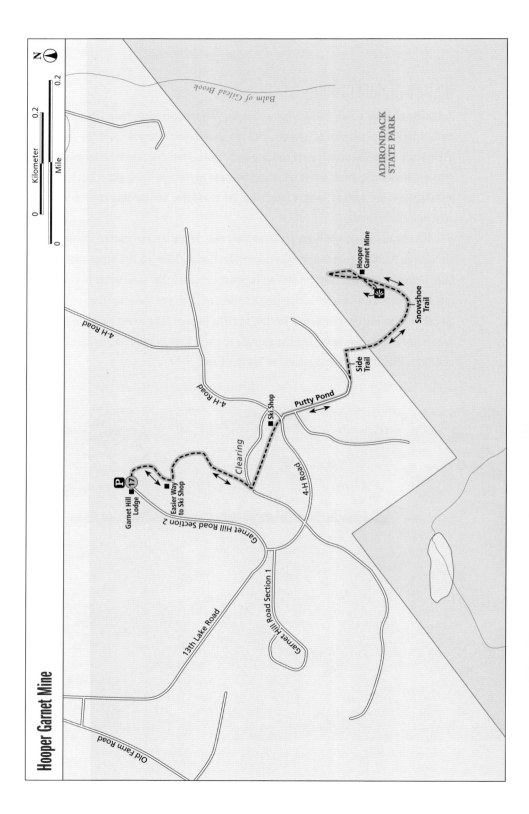

N

Kilometer
0   0.2

Mile
0   0.2

Balm of Gilead Brook

ADIRONDACK
STATE PARK

Hooper
Garnet Mine

Snowshoe
Trail

Side
Trail

Putty Pond

Ski Shop

Clearing

4-H Road

4-H Road

P
17
Garnet Hill
Lodge

Easier Way
to Ski Shop

Garnet Hill Road Section 2

Garnet Hill Road Section 1

13th Lake Road

Old Farm Road

0.2 Emerge in a clearing. Go straight to get to the ski shop.

0.3 Reach the ski shop (the Mild to Wild Adventure Center). Pass it and take the trail labeled "Putty Pond," straight ahead as you come into the clearing. Follow the sign to the Hooper Mine. (The tennis courts will be on your right as you enter the woods.) Just before the trail bends left, a side trail appears to your right. Go right, and immediately turn onto the snowshoe trail, indicated with yellow-and-black markers.

0.4 Turn right at the fork and start going up.

0.7 Reach the top, where you can see big reddish rock faces across the meadow. Make your way through the vigorous vegetation to the rocks, where you will see the glitter of gemstones embedded in the rock faces. On the west side of the clearing, climb up the pile of rocks to the ridge for a spectacular view of the High Peaks region. When you're ready, return the way you came.

1.4 Arrive back at Garnet Hill Lodge.

From Hooper Garnet Mine, you can enjoy a view of the surrounding mountains.

18 OK Slip Falls

After many years of waiting, we can now see the tallest waterfall in New York State at the end of a trail through a former logging district.

Start: Parking area on NY 28 between North Creek and Indian Lake
Distance: 6.4 miles out and back, including the walk from the parking area to the trailhead
Hiking time: About 4 hours
Elevation gain: 331 feet
High point: 1,937 feet
Difficulty: Moderate
Best season: Summer and fall

Traffic: Hikers only
Fees and permits: No fees or permits required
Maps: Available online at www.dec.ny.gov/docs/regions_pdf/okslptrailmp.pdf
Trail contacts: New York State Department of Environmental Conservation (NYSDEC), Region 5, 1115 NY 86, Ray Brook 12977; (518) 897-1200; www.dec.ny.gov

Finding the trailhead: The trail begins on NY 28 between North Creek and Indian Lake. From the intersection of NY 28 and NY 30 in Indian Lake, drive 7.5 miles east on NY 28 to the parking area. Look for the brown DEC sign and the paved parking area on the south side of the road.

From North Creek, drive about 4 miles west on NY 28 to find the parking area. GPS: N43 46.262' / W74 08.024'

The Hike

By Adirondack standards, the 3-mile (one way) trail to OK Slip Falls is a walk in the park with a big, big payoff: the first close-up views hikers have ever had of the tallest waterfall in New York State. Cascading 250 feet, this magnificent waterfall suddenly appears as you come off a pair of switchbacks at the end of the trail, a sight that had been denied hikers for more than a century as a large corporation held private ownership of this land.

Purchased by the Adirondack Nature Conservancy in 2007 and sold to New York State in 2013, OK Slip Falls and the surrounding 161,000 acres are now part of the Hudson Gorge Wilderness Area. It took another year for the state to complete this well-marked, nicely maintained trail—one just rugged enough to feel like an adventurous hike while easy enough for families to bring their children to see the spectacle of falling water.

Nearly the first mile of the trail may seem familiar to some veteran Adirondack hikers: It's the trail to Ross Pond, a nice reuse of an already well-traveled route. From the junction less than 1 mile from the OK Slip trailhead, the Student Conservation Society of the Department of Environmental Conservation (DEC) built the new trail to OK Slip Falls without having to remove any mature trees.

Historical Background

Logging in the Adirondacks began as far back as the 1600s, when English settlers took over the land from the Dutch. England recognized the profit opportunity the vast forests of upstate New York presented, and began harvesting trees for use in building homes and towns. When the land became part of the new America's holdings after the Revolutionary War, the forests of the Adirondack region offered one of the fastest ways for the state to discharge its war debts. The state welcomed the lumber industry with open arms, giving logging companies full access to more than 7 million acres of old-growth forests. While the lumber industry focused on pine, the arrival of the paper industry (including Finch Pruyn, the company that owned the land that contains the OK Slip Falls trail) meant that spruce and fir trees fell as well, and the tanning industry clear-cut the hemlock woods. The vast forests disappeared, leaving open land for farms and towns.

By the 1850s the state had begun to see the error of its ways. With so many trees removed and thousands of acres of land denuded, the soil became so porous that it could no longer hold rainwater. Floods and topsoil erosion became significant hazards. The condition of the formerly forested land became so dire that the state finally determined that these lands required special protection and reforestation.

The result is Adirondack Park, signed into law in 1894 and protected as "forever wild" in perpetuity. Some sustainable logging still goes on in this area, but under strict guidelines that preserve forested land while shepherding replacement growth of the trees removed by the industry.

Miles and Directions

0.0 Start from the parking area and walk up NY 28 to the trailhead on the north side of the road. When you reach the trailhead, hop over the guardrail wire and head downhill to the trail. Stop at the trail registry and register before following the bright red trail markers.

0.9 At the intersection with the Ross Pond Trail, leave the red-marked trail and follow the blue markers to your right.

2.3 A private road crosses the trail. Turn left and walk along the road to the next trail junction. Turn right at the sign and the blue marker, and continue on the trail.

2.5 Cross a nicely built new bridge over a stream.

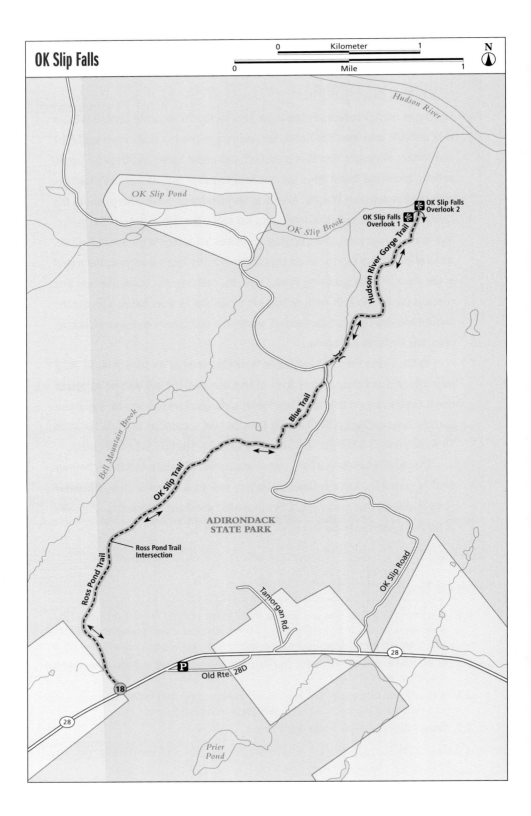

OK Slip Falls

OK Slip Pond

Hudson River

OK Slip Brook

OK Slip Falls
Overlook 1

OK Slip Falls
Overlook 2

Hudson River Gorge Trail

Blue Trail

OK Slip Trail

Bell Mountain Brook

ADIRONDACK
STATE PARK

Ross Pond Trail
Intersection

Ross Pond Trail

OK Slip Road

Tamorgan Rd.

P

Old Rte. 28D

28

18

28

Prier
Pond

The DEC built and maintains this trail to OK Slip Falls and Hudson River Gorge.

View OK Slip Falls from the safety of this rock ledge.

How OK Slip Got Its Name

While most New Yorkers would not consider working outside on an icy pond in the dead of winter, the frictionless coating on the pond here at the top of Hudson River Gorge actually served the logging industry well. From 1900 to 1922, lumberjacks used the ice to pile up logs from the Adirondack wilderness to await their trip to the Hudson River, where they would float to waiting railroad cars and barges far downstream.

The logs would wait on the ice behind a dam until the spring thaw, when logging men would release water and logs through the dam and down a chute, or slip, at the northwest corner of the pond. Just as they released the logs, they yelled, "OK, slip!" to the waiting hands below. The water and logs tumbled down the slip and into the river for their trip out of the mountains.

While the logs didn't come down the waterfall—at least, not intentionally—the falls took the name of the pond and brook that were critical parts of the log transportation system.

3.1 At the intersection with the Hudson River Gorge Trail, turn right.

3.2 Reach the first overlook, where you can see OK Slip Falls and the 270-foot-deep gorge. The trail continues to your right to a second overlook, where the trail ends. When you're ready, return the way you came.

6.4 Arrive back at the parking area.

19 John Brown Farm State Historic Site

The home of the anti-slavery activist who led the raid on Harpers Ferry offers a tranquil respite from the crowds in nearby Lake Placid.

Start: Parking area at John Brown State Historic Site, Lake Placid
Distance: 1.0-mile loop
Hiking time: About 45 minutes, with stops at the historic buildings and gravesites
Elevation gain: 101 feet
High point: 1,899 feet
Difficulty: Easy
Best season: Spring through fall
Traffic: Hikers, cyclists

Fees and permits: Nominal fee for touring the grounds during peak season (Memorial Day through Labor Day)
Maps: Available online at nysparks.com/historic-sites/attachments/JohnBrownFarm TrailMap.pdf
Trail contacts: John Brown Farm State Historic Site, 115 John Brown Rd., Lake Placid 12946; (518) 523-3900; nysparks.com/historic-sites/29/details.aspx

Finding the trailhead: From Lake Placid take NY 73 south/east about 1.8 miles to SR 910M (John Brown Road). Bear left at the intersection onto John Brown Road, and continue to the state historic site. Park in the gravel lot just before the traffic circle. GPS: N44 15.097' / W73 58.282'

The Hike

This easy loop ambles through two significant pieces of history: John Brown's farm, the home of one of the most passionate defenders of the right of black slaves to be free men and women; and the impressive ski jump structures built for the 1980 Winter Olympics.

The tour of the farm property wanders through an open meadow filled with wildflowers throughout spring and summer, and then through a fragrant woodland. Birders can find some of the local specialties on this property, including black-backed and American three-toed woodpeckers, species that New York birders travel north specifically to see.

The ski jumps are still in use today by skiers training for national and international competitions, but even if you're not a world-class skier, you can tour the ski jump complex and see the view from the top of the higher jump. If the height seems daunting (or terrifying), you can enjoy the impressive sight of the two towers from this trail.

Abolitionist John Brown lived on this humble farm until his death in 1859.

John Brown Farm State Historic Site

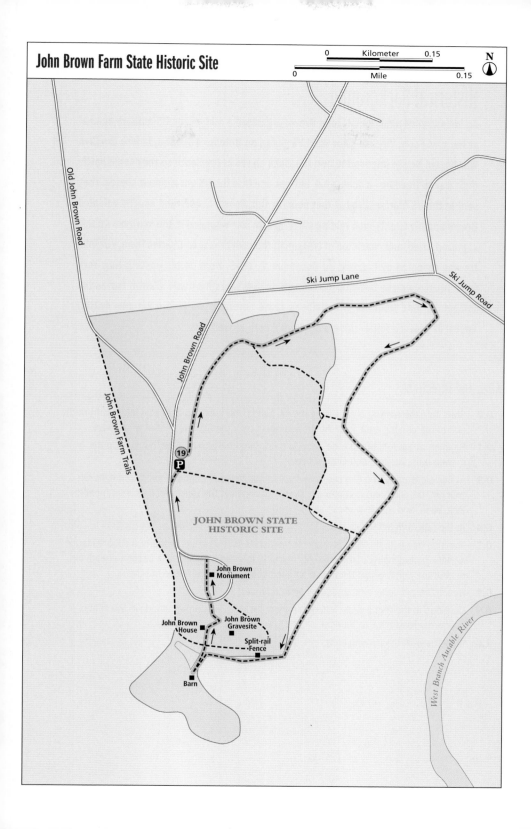

Historical Background

An impassioned abolitionist, John Brown organized a raid on the US military arsenal at Harpers Ferry, Virginia (now West Virginia), on October 16, 1859, before the Civil War began. Brown intended to arm the black slaves in the South so they could battle their way to freedom—a noble goal, but not one that the US government shared. They sent in the US Marines—led at that point by Col. Robert E. Lee—and handily defeated Brown and his twenty-man raiding party. Brown was wounded in the marines' attack, captured, tried, and convicted of treason in the courthouse in Charles Town, Virginia. He was executed by hanging on December 2, 1859. Here on his upstate New York farm, his remains lie beneath the tombstone that bears his name. (Brown moved the tombstone here from his grandfather's grave several years before his own death.) Twelve of Brown's fellow raiders are buried here as well.

Miles and Directions

0.0 Start from the parking area. Facing the ski jumps, the trailhead is to your left (north) at the end of the parking area. Take the mowed-grass path through the field of wildflowers.

0.1 Bear left at the fork of the wide, mowed path. Other trails cross here, but stay on the mowed path. The trail enters the woods.

0.3 At this crossroads, you can see snowmaking machines through the trees. Turn right. On your left, the Ski Jump Complex is visible. In a moment the trail turns right into the hemlock, birch, and maple woods.

0.4 At the fork, turn left.

0.7 The blue house to the right is a private residence. Just past this property, a split-rail fence signals the beginning of the state historic site. John Brown's house is straight ahead. Turn right at the pond to visit the house and cemetery, or turn left to see the barn.

0.8 Reach the gravesite, surrounded by an iron fence.

0.9 Continue to the traffic circle, where the monument to John Brown stands in the center. Follow the road back to your car.

1.0 Arrive back at the parking area.

20 Paul Smith's College: Heron Marsh Trail

This oasis of native species, well-groomed trails, and pristine open space provides a rare and delightful hiking treat.

Start: Visitor Interpretive Center (VIC) at Paul Smith's College
Distance: 3.0-mile loop
Hiking time: About 2 hours
Elevation gain: 142 feet
High point: 1,723 feet
Difficulty: Easy
Best season: Spring through fall

Traffic: Hikers, cross-country skiers and snowshoers, anglers
Fees and permits: Winter trail fees cover the cost of grooming the trails.
Maps: Available online at adirondackvic.org/TrailMap.html
Trail contacts: Paul Smith's College VIC, 8023 NY 30, Paul Smith's 12970; (518) 327-6241; adirondackvic.org

Finding the trailhead: From the town of Tupper Lake, take NY 3/30 north for 6 miles until the two routes split; turn left onto NY 30 toward Paul Smith's College. Continue 21 miles to Paul Smith's College, and drive 1 mile past the college to the VIC. The entrance is on the left side of NY 30. Park and walk through the VIC building to the trailheads, and follow the signs for the Heron Marsh Trail. GPS: N44 26.976' / W74 15.547'

The Hike

A testament to sustainable land management and the eradication of invasive species, this trail shows us what New York must have looked like before Europeans arrived with their exotic plants, hitchhiking seeds, and inexplicable attachment to house sparrows.

The Heron Marsh Trail wanders through one exquisite landscape after another, from hardwood and mixed conifer-hardwood forests to pristine wetlands, where pickerelweed and blue flag iris do not have to fight against purple loosestrife and Queen Anne's lace for a foothold. You may see plants here that you've only read about in books, native species that once thrived in New York. Visit here more than once over a range of seasons, and see the forest floor and the expansive wetlands change and bloom with new colors and varieties.

Birds and animals thrive here as well, and this trail features some prime viewing areas, including a tower from which you can watch for great blue heron, common loon, common merganser, wood and ring-necked ducks, American bittern, and smaller birds like common yellowthroat, swamp sparrow, and ovenbird. You almost certainly will spot white-tailed deer in the woods, and animals including eastern chipmunk, groundhog, gray and red squirrels, and other woodland creatures are common sights here.

Historical Background

Training "stewards of the Earth" since 1946, Paul Smith's College is best known for its School of Natural Resource Management and Ecology, where the next generation of environmental scientists and park managers learn skills they will use for a lifetime. The college offers degrees in environmental science, fisheries and wildlife science, forestry, natural resource management and sustainability, and park and recreation management.

How did this college within a park come to be? Back in 1859, Apollos "Paul" Smith and his wife, Lydia, built a hotel on 50,000 acres of land they purchased on Lower St. Regis Lake—the first wilderness resort in the Adirondacks. As the resort grew, its reputation expanded as well, welcoming three presidents of the United States among its most illustrious guests. Paul Smith died in 1912, and his son, Phelps, continued to run the resort; but when it was destroyed in a massive fire in 1930, Phelps decided to bequeath the land to found a college that would honor his father's love of the Adirondacks and the vast wilderness around his property. Phelps Smith also left a large sum of money to be used to found the college, ensuring that it would actually come to be.

Paul Smith's College welcomed its first class in 1946, providing higher education to a number of World War II veterans as well as local graduates of area high schools. Today Paul Smith's is the only four-year college in Adirondack Park, offering students hands-on learning opportunities that make its graduates especially valuable to parks, wildlife refuges, and open spaces of all kinds, both in New York and across the country.

The VIC offers thirteen trails in addition to this one, so if you love the Heron Marsh Trail as much as we did, you may want to try out some of the others. In particular, the 1-mile Boreal Life Trail presents much of what makes the Adirondacks such an unusual place, with a 1,600-foot boardwalk through a mountain bog and a conifer forest along a lovely pond. Here you may see boreal chickadee, black-backed woodpecker, and gray jay, three of the local specialties you may need for your New York life list.

The well-groomed trails at Paul Smith's College VIC offer some of the best day hiking in the Adirondacks.

Paul Smith's College: Heron Marsh Trail

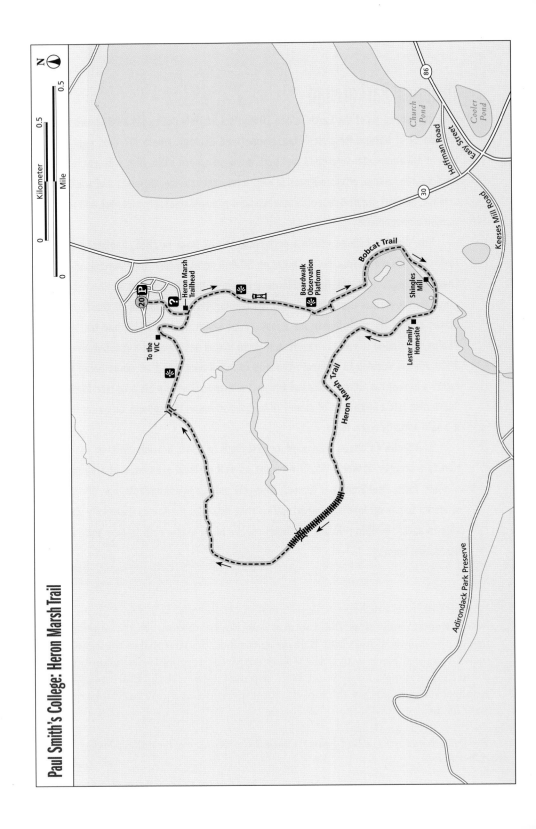

Miles and Directions

0.0 Start from the parking area and walk to the VIC building; go through the building to the trailheads behind it. Follow the gray signs for the Heron Marsh Trail.

0.1 Bear right at the first intersection. At the four-way intersection ahead, continue straight. Follow the gray trail markers.

0.3 The boardwalk goes right here for a view of the marsh and the surrounding mountains. As you return from the boardwalk, a lean-to is visible through the hemlocks. Turn right and continue on the trail.

0.4 Come to the observation tower.

0.5 A boardwalk leads to an observation platform to the left. In summer you'll see water lilies (the white flowers) and yellow pond lilies blooming here. When you return to the trail, the second lean-to is on your left. Continue straight.

What Are Invasive Species?

Species of plants, animals, and microorganisms that are not native to a specific region may become invasive—causing harm to the economy, environment, and/or human health. In the Adirondacks, aquatic invasive species are particularly pernicious, choking waterways with plants and underwater animals that do not belong in these lakes and rivers. Invasive species can make it impossible for native plants and animals to survive in these waters, killing off important food supplies for birds, fish, and mammals and disturbing the waterways' natural ability to keep themselves clean and pure.

If you've taken a boat out on Saranac Lake or wandered along the shoreline of just about any Adirondack waterway, you've seen some of these species: the white flowers of the European frog-bit on a lake's surface; tangles of Eurasian watermilfoil, a submersed plant with feather-like leaves; curly-leafed pondweed appearing reddish-brown below the surface; tiny Asian clams, each of which can produce 35,000 offspring in a single season; and the dark-colored zebra mussels that also propagate in the Great Lakes. These species hitchhike into the Adirondacks on the hulls of boats or the propellers of outboard motors, or even on the soles of hiking boots. You can help keep these species from spreading further by checking your clothing and shoes before and after you hike, especially near any body of water, and use the receptacles at boat docks to leave behind trailing plant fragments or shellfish that cling to your boat when you remove it from the water.

Water lily, a New York native plant, finds the right habitat at Paul Smith's College.

0.6 To your right, a boardwalk goes across the marsh on the Woods and Waters Trail. While the Heron Marsh Trail doesn't go that way, it's well worth walking out onto this boardwalk for a broad view of the marsh. When you're ready, return to the trail and continue straight.

0.8 At the junction with the Bobcat Trail, continue straight.

1.0 Reach the site of the former Shingles Mill. There's a small waterfall here. Cross the bridge over the waterfall, and turn right at the intersection with Loggers' Loop.

1.1 Reach the former homesite of the Lester family. Interpretive signs here tell you more about them.

1.5 At the intersection with the Woods and Waters Trail, turn right.

1.7 A boardwalk begins here, crossing a new forest.

1.9 The boardwalk ends as you enter an Adirondack hardwood forest.

2.1 At the intersection, turn right onto the Heron Marsh Trail (not on the Jenkins Mountain Trail).

2.5 Turn right at the sign for the Interpretive Building. Cross a bridge.

2.6 Come to a viewing platform.

2.8 At the intersection with Barnum Brook Loop, bear right. Turn right again at the sign that says "To the VIC."

3.0 Arrive back at the VIC building. You may want to enjoy the displays here or visit the gift shop before returning to your vehicle.

21 Tahawus Ghost Town

Tucked into a remote corner of Adirondack Park, this short hike tells a meaty story about ironworking and elite hunting.

Start: Near the High Peaks trailhead for Indian Pass, Lake Colden Dam, Duck Hole, and Mt. Marcy, at the end of CR 25 (Upper Works Road) in Tahawus. Set your GPS to the intersection of Upper Works Road and Santononi Road, and turn left (north) on Upper Works Road.
Distance: 1.4 miles out and back
Hiking time: About 45 minutes
Elevation gain: 71 feet
High point: 1,803 feet

Difficulty: Easy
Best season: Summer and fall
Traffic: Hikers, limited motor vehicle traffic
Fees and permits: No fees or permits required
Maps: Available online at visitadirondacks .com/hiking/adirondac-tahawus-mines
Trail contacts: Open Space Institute, Airline Plaza, 1350 Broadway #201, New York 10018; (212) 290-8200; osiny.org

Finding the trailhead: From the town of Newcomb in Essex County, take NY 28N east/south to CR 76 and turn left. Continue on CR 76 as it joins CR 25; keep going for about 2.5 miles. Watch for the interpretive displays on your right for the Adirondac Iron Works. Park here along the road and walk to the displays. GPS: N44 05.280' / W74 03.364'

The Hike

More of a stroll than a hike, this amble through the ruins of an ironworks and (later) vacation resort is packed with fascinating Adirondack history. It begins at the remains of the Adirondac Iron Works and moves up the road at a leisurely pace, giving you the opportunity to peer into the handful of broken buildings that remain and wonder about the people who once labored at this remote industrial site—and the circumstances that led an American vice president to make a famous midnight ride out of the mountains in a horse-drawn carriage.

The Open Space Institute, which took control of this property in 2003, has provided interpretive signs and displays that guide you through the ironworks. The sturdy furnace you see here has already survived for more than 150 years in remarkably fresh condition, while the wheelhouse and other structures have fared somewhat less successfully over time. Imagine this place bustling with as many as 400 workers, and you may have a sense of the difficulty processing iron on this rugged land posed for the owners and their rough-and-ready workforce.

The buildings along the road, only one of which has enjoyed the benefit of a significant renovation, are actually the remains of the Tahawus Club, the vacation resort that inhabited this area beginning in the late nineteenth century. Explore the inside of these ruins at your own risk, but you can view their innards from the outside

Historical Background

A ghost town in the Adirondacks—what can that be like? If you're expecting tumble-weeds and posts where a cowpoke once tied up his horse, you may need to adjust your mental picture. The tiny town of Tahawus has its share of ramshackle structures that have fallen in on themselves, but it never saw cowboys or shootouts at high noon.

This northeastern ghost town once bustled with the activity of the Adirondac Iron Works, an operation that processed as much as 12 to 14 tons of iron ore daily during its heyday in the 1840s. As many as 400 workers once ran the equipment you can still see here, from the massive McIntyre furnace to the machinery used to harness waterpower in the wheelhouse.

Adirondac actually had two heydays: one for two years in the mid-1840s and another in 1854. Iron from the Adirondacks made the best steel, according to experts in the steel-manufacturing industry, so pig iron from this area sold for as much as twice the amount per ton that other American ironworks operations received. The difficulty, however, was in bringing the iron down from this remote mountain setting to the steel mills to the south. After two years of intense work to bring a railroad up to Adirondac, the owners finally had to face the fact that the time-consuming, labor-intensive, innately hazardous process of transporting the iron ore over inadequate roads had taken its toll on the business. The ironworks ceased to run.

Roughly nine years later, hope returned to the beleaguered iron operation. The Sackett's Harbor and Saratoga Railroad Company expressed real interest in running its line to the village of Adirondac to transport the valuable ore out of the mountains. With great excitement and near certainty that the railroad was on its way, the owners performed a costly renovation of the existing buildings, including construction of a new blast furnace—an out-of-pocket expense of an astronomical $43,000. As time went on and the railroad did not begin construction of the spur to Adirondac, however, the owners eventually realized that there would be no railroad. In 1857 the owners deserted the Adirondac Iron Works.

While the remote location inhibited the ironworks' ability to thrive, another kind of operation found this the perfect place to be. The Preston Ponds Club opened its doors in 1876, leasing these buildings from what had become the Adirondack Iron and Steel Company. Hunters and anglers frequented this club, often bringing their families for a vacation retreat at the headwaters of the Hudson River. Within a year, the new club had incorporated and changed its name to the Adirondack Club, and eventually it settled on the name that lingers to this day: the Tahawus Club.

The renovated building you see here served as a lodge at the hunting club, and it holds a unique place in history. Here in September 1901, Vice President Theodore Roosevelt vacationed with his family while President William McKinley received medical care in Buffalo after anarchist Leon Czolgosz shot him at the Pan-American Exposition. Roosevelt had heard from officials in Buffalo that the president would make a speedy recovery, so the vice president felt comfortable making an overnight hike up Mount Marcy with family and friends. By the time Roosevelt returned to Tahawus the following day, he found a messenger waiting for him. McKinley had taken a turn for the worse.

As the president neared death, Roosevelt made a 35-mile carriage ride through the night to the nearest railroad depot, in North Creek, but by the time he reached the train station, he learned that McKinley had passed away. Roosevelt took a train to Albany and another from there to Buffalo, arriving at about 1:30 p.m. Two hours later, on September 14, 1901, Federal District Judge John Hazel swore Roosevelt in as president of the United States.

All that remains of Tahawus mining town is a handful of dilapidated buildings at the end of the road.

Inside, the ghost buildings show their age and workmanship.

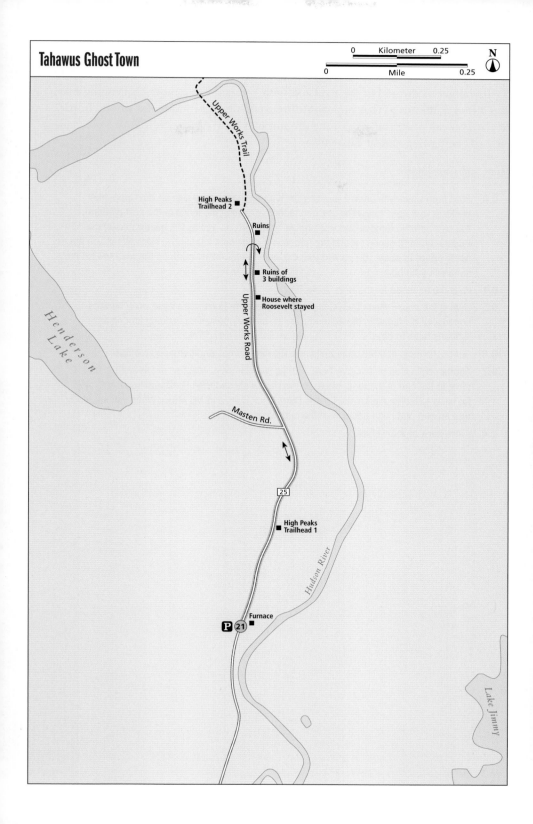

Tahawus Ghost Town

0 Kilometer 0.25
0 Mile 0.25

N

Upper Works Trail

High Peaks
Trailhead 2

Ruins

Ruins of
3 buildings

House where
Roosevelt stayed

Upper Works Road

Henderson Lake

Masten Rd.

25

High Peaks
Trailhead 1

Hudson River

Furnace

P 21

Lake Jimmy

through gaping windows and doorways to get a sense of time's toll on the century-old structures.

If you get to the end of the road and wish you had had a more challenging hike, you'll find trailheads to four popular Adirondack hikes just inside the woods. In particular, you can make the hike to the summit of Mount Marcy, New York State's tallest peak, beginning here at Tahawus.

Miles and Directions

0.0 Start from where you parked your vehicle. With the interpretive sign for the Upper Iron Works at your right, follow the crushed-stone path along the fence to the next platform. You can view the furnace and wheelhouse from here, as well as the headwaters of the Hudson River. Continue around the furnace for additional interpretive signs. When you are ready, return to where you parked your car, and begin walking north on the road toward the remains of the buildings.

0.1 Pass the trailhead for the High Peaks Trail.

0.5 Here is the house where then vice president Theodore Roosevelt stayed while he vacationed with his family in the Adirondacks. It's the only preserved building among the Tahawus ruins to date.

0.6 Reach the ruins of three other buildings. They are homes and perhaps an office.

0.7 Another collapsed building lay here, with its two chimneys intact as of this writing. Continue to the end of the road, where you will see a second High Peaks trailhead—this one for hikes to Indian Pass, Lake Colden Dam, Duck Hole, and Mt. Marcy. When you are ready, turn around and head back down the road to your vehicle.

1.4 Arrive back at your vehicle.

22 Crown Point State Historic Site to Vermont

Walk the path to two eighteenth-century forts that tell two distinctly different stories—and top off your hike with a lake crossing to Vermont.

Start: Paved path in front of the visitor center and museum at the state historic site
Distance: 2.4 miles round-trip
Hiking time: About 1.25 hours
Elevation gain: 105 feet
High point: 191 feet
Difficulty: Easy
Best season: Spring through fall
Traffic: Hikers only

Fees and permits: Entrance fee, paid at the museum
Maps: Available online at nysparks.com/historic-sites/34/maps.aspx
Trail contacts: Crown Point State Historic Site, 21 Grandview Dr., Crown Point 12928; (518) 597-3666; nysparks.com/historic-sites/34/details.aspx

Finding the trailhead: From Albany take the Northway (I-87) north about 125 miles to exit 28. From the exit take NY 74 East toward Ticonderoga. In about 17 miles turn left onto NY 22. In about 8 miles turn right onto Lake Road. Stay on Lake Road for 3.5 miles until you reach NY 185 East. Turn right onto NY 185 and follow the signs to Crown Point State Historic Site. GPS: N44 01.793' / W73 25.647'

The Hike

Here at the pivot point between French and English domination of this peninsula on the edge of Lake Champlain, the remains of two forts tell a compelling story of military life before the Revolutionary War. This trail gives you ample opportunity to explore both forts, marvel at the fact that these stone walls still stand more than 250 years after their construction, and take in the view soldiers may have paused to enjoy between battles.

Paved paths, stone steps, and sloping earthworks make this an interesting hike as well as an informative one.

No walk at Crown Point would be complete without crossing the Lake Champlain Bridge into Chimney Point, Vermont. This new span was built almost entirely offsite in Port Henry and brought here by barge for final placement in 2011. The bridge replaced the failing Champlain Bridge—deemed irreparably damaged by time in 2009. To keep the surrounding area from the economic hardships of a long-term bridge closure, the states of New York and Vermont joined forces to construct a new bridge in less than two years' time. Today the gently arching expanse provides a dedicated pedestrian walkway, giving you the pleasure of strolling over the bridge at your leisure and enjoying the panoramic view of Lake Champlain and the New York and Vermont shorelines.

Historical Background

From explorer Samuel de Champlain's arrival in 1609 to the British retreat in 1775, three different governments viewed Crown Point as a prized possession for control of this narrow point on this important waterway. The channel, now crossed easily via the Lake Champlain Bridge, offered a critical defense point in securing the land beyond—first for the French, then for the British, and lastly for the newly formed United States. Control of the channel also meant control of trade between two early centers of commerce: New York to the south and Montreal to the north.

The French planted their flag and occupied this point in 1731, and in 1734 they completed construction of Fort St. Frederic, the older of the two forts you see on this hike. Here merchants and farmers joined the soldiers on the point, establishing a community around the protection of the military. The fort provided a doctor, hospital, chapel, and flour mill, while the surrounding village provided food and livestock products. The French military brought the first sailing vessel to the lake as well—a 50-foot sloop called *La Vigilante*.

When the British arrived in force in 1755, the French were fortified and ready to fight. Again and again from 1755 to 1758, the British attacked Fort St. Frederic and attempted to oust the French army, but the soldiers and villagers resisted and turned back the British forces. Finally, in 1759, the French got wind of an impending attack by British forces too numerous and powerful for them to beat in battle. The French soldiers and villagers decided to retreat, demolishing their fort and leaving little the British would find useful once they took control of the point. French lives were saved even as their holdings were lost.

The British settled in and built their own fort, naming it Fort Crown Point and bringing in as many as 3,000 workers to construct one of the largest star forts in colonial North America. Here the living quarters could house up to 500 people, while a village to the southwest of the fort provided housing for retired soldiers and some living with their families. The British troops remained in relative peace until a fire broke out in a chimney in the soldiers' barracks in April 1773, leading military engineer John Montresor to describe it as "an amazing useless mass of Earth only." The British vacated the fort soon after, leaving a small cadre to guard it—and they fell in short order when one hundred Green Mountain Boys under the command of Capt. Seth Warner attacked them on May 12, 1775. The Americans took the fort and 111 cannons, and the British presence at Crown Point came to an end.

Miles and Directions

0.0 Start in front of the museum. Walk northeast toward the ruins of the French fort. In about 100 feet, reach an interpretive sign about Fort St. Frederic. Leave the path and walk across the grass to interpretive sign #1 at the fort entrance.

0.1 Enter the fort ruins. Keeping the structure to your right, circle the inside of the fort to interpretive signs #3, #4, #5, and #6. There's a fine view of the bridge and the lake from here. As you leave the fort, walk straight out to interpretive stop #7 for the best view yet of the lake.

0.2 Turn around and take the stone path and/or sidewalk to the British fort.

0.3 Turn right and head southwest toward the British fort. Just past the parking area, stop at the interpretive sign at the earthwork fortifications.

0.4 There's a gate on the road to your left. In front of you is stop #9 on the fort tour. You are entering the ruins of Fort Crown Point, the British fort (1759–73). As you come into the fort, you can see tour stop #10 on your left. Continue straight to the next interpretive sign.

0.5 At the interpretive sign about the barracks, you may want to detour from this route and explore the inside of the fort. When you are ready to continue, take the stairs to the right up the earthworks. At the top you have an excellent view of the Adirondack foothills and

The forts and Lake Champlain views make a visit to Crown Point especially satisfying.

Crown Point State Historic Site to Vermont

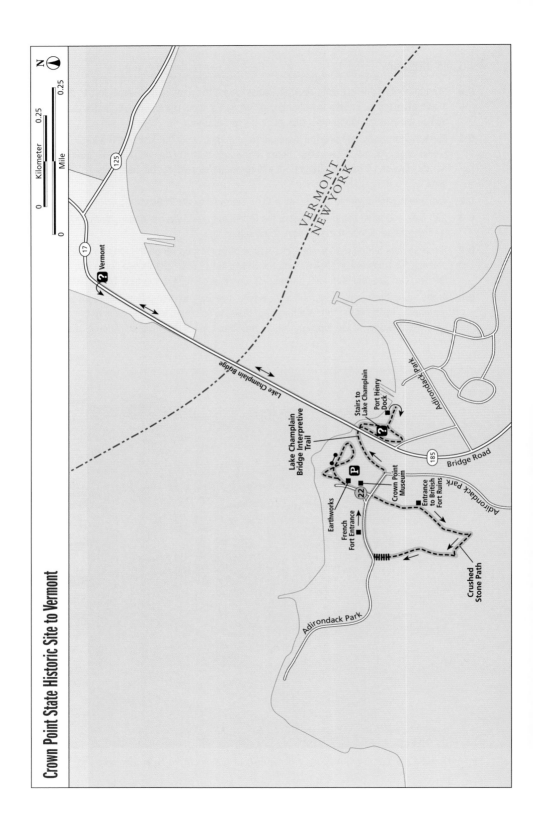

Lake Champlain (behind you). When you're ready, head back down the stairs and turn right on the path; continue to stop #12.

0.6 Earthworks are on your left, revetments on your right. In the middle, you can see the ditch. Stop #13 explains its significance and other details about life at the fort. Turn left and walk down through the ditch.

0.7 At the east end of the fort, at stop #14, you rejoin the sidewalk. Turn right and walk to the bridge. Take the crushed-stone path of the Lake Champlain Bridge Interpretive Trail. Signs along this route provide information about the history of the bridge. The path takes you down to the water's edge and under the bridge.

0.9 Reach Port Henry Dock. Straight ahead and to the left is the Champlain Memorial Lighthouse. When you've had a good viewing, retrace your steps to the stairs that lead up to the Lake Champlain Visitor Center. Walk up the driveway to the road, and turn right to cross the bridge.

Lake Champlain Bridge offers an easy walking and driving route to Vermont.

1.1 Reach the beginning of the bridge on the New York side. Walk across.

1.6 The bridge crossing ends at Vermont's Chimney Point Visitor Center. Recross the bridge and head back toward the museum and parking area.

2.4 Arrive back at the Crown Point museum and parking area.

Catskill Region

In the Catskills, you can see the views that artists of the Hudson River School captured on canvas.

23 Upper Delaware River / Roebling Bridge

Take in the views of a National Scenic and Recreational River at its most admired and celebrated crossing.

Start: Delaware Aqueduct on NY 97 between Tusten and Barryville, near the junction with CR 168.
Distance: 1.7 miles out and back
Hiking time: About 30 minutes
Elevation gain: 125 feet
High point: 627 feet
Difficulty: Easy
Best season: Spring through fall
Traffic: Hikers, cyclists

Fees and permits: No fees or permits required
Maps: Available at nps.gov/upde
Trail contacts: Upper Delaware National Scenic and Recreational River, 274 River Rd., Beach Lake, PA 18405; (570) 685-4871; nps .gov/upde
Special considerations: If you plan to include a visit to the Zane Gray Museum, call ahead at (570) 685-4871 to be sure it will be open on the day of your visit.

Finding the trailhead: From NY 17 (I-86), take exit 87 for Hancock. At the end of the exit ramp, follow NY 97 East for 48 miles to the Roebling Bridge / Delaware Aqueduct (watch for the National Park Service signs after Tusten). Park in the designated area at the bridge; the trailhead is at the west end of the parking area. GPS: N41 28.900' / W74 58.958'

The Hike

What this brisk walk lacks in challenge it definitely makes up in scenic beauty, with the added boost of technological ingenuity. Here you have the opportunity to see and walk across the oldest existing wire cable suspension bridge in the United States, one that once carried the waters of the Delaware and Hudson Canal over another waterway, the Upper Delaware River.

Park in the area provided at the bridge and begin your walk at the clearly marked trailhead. Walk east along the gentle river for 0.5 mile to Minisink Ford, location of a hamlet that became the site of a Revolutionary War battle in 1779. The short trail ends here, so once you've enjoyed the view and perhaps a picnic lunch, you'll turn around and walk back to the Roebling Bridge. At this point, it's only natural to turn onto the bridge and cross into Pennsylvania. If you'd like to extend your walk, the Zane Gray Museum, former home of the legendary author of more than ninety books that created the Western genre—most notably *Riders of the Purple Sage*, his best-selling work—is just 0.4 mile west of the bridge on Scenic Drive in Lackawaxen, Pennsylvania.

Historical Background

Engineer John A. Roebling designed this aqueduct, a key element in the Delaware and Hudson (D&H) Canal and Gravity Railroad, to speed the transportation of anthracite coal from northeastern Pennsylvania to the Hudson River. So respected was Roebling's work on this aqueduct and other such projects, he became the engineer of choice for much larger projects—including his crowning achievement, the Brooklyn Bridge.

The Delaware Aqueduct replaced a slack-water dam—a structure that formed a pool of slow-moving water in the middle of the river to allow boats to cross the river safely. Mules and their drivers crossed using a rope ferry, a process that slowed traffic on the Delaware River and made it virtually impossible for the D&H Canal to compete with its faster transportation rivals—especially the railroads, which in the 1840s were gaining power, frequency, and speed.

The aqueduct opened in 1848 and alleviated the slack-water bottleneck, making the D&H Canal competitive once again. Roebling's ingenious design allowed ice floes and river traffic to pass under the bridge easily, while taking barges and other boats across the river from above. With the aqueduct in place, the D&H Canal sustained operations for fifty years, until the canal's closure in 1898.

In 1968 the Department of the Interior designated the Delaware Aqueduct a National Historic Landmark, making it eligible for protection and ripe for restoration. When the National Park Service bought the aqueduct in 1980, it had become a vehicle bridge and had fallen into disrepair. The park service supervised a restoration that included reconstruction of the superstructure according to Roebling's initial plans, while preserving the original ironwork in place. All the cables, saddles, and suspenders are the ones originally installed in 1848. The park service notes that the two suspension cables were spun on-site under Roebling's direction back in 1847, tested for viability during the restoration and found to be sturdy enough to remain in place. Today the bridge looks much as it did in 1848, making it an enduring and useful landmark along the New York–Pennsylvania border.

The Roebling Bridge provides a short walking route to Pennsylvania.

Miles and Directions

0.0 Start at the trailhead at the west end of the parking area. Follow the trail around to the east and along the river to Minisink Ford.

0.4 The trail ends; return the way you came.

Upper Delaware Scenic and Recreational River

Many New Yorkers react with surprise when they drive NY 97 and discover a unit of the National Park Service here on the Pennsylvania border. The Upper Delaware Scenic and Recreational River protects 73.4 miles of pristine river, uninterrupted by dams or other man-made means of entrapping its waters. The river supplied human beings with a freshwater supply as far back as 15,000 BCE, and later became a key transportation tool in bringing logs, anthracite, and bluestone out of the Catskills and into the state's industrial centers. Even today, the river supplies more than 17 million people with drinking water, while more than 500,000 visitors annually enjoy its recreational merits, from fishing and hunting to float trips down its quiet waters.

Upper Delaware River/Roebling Bridge

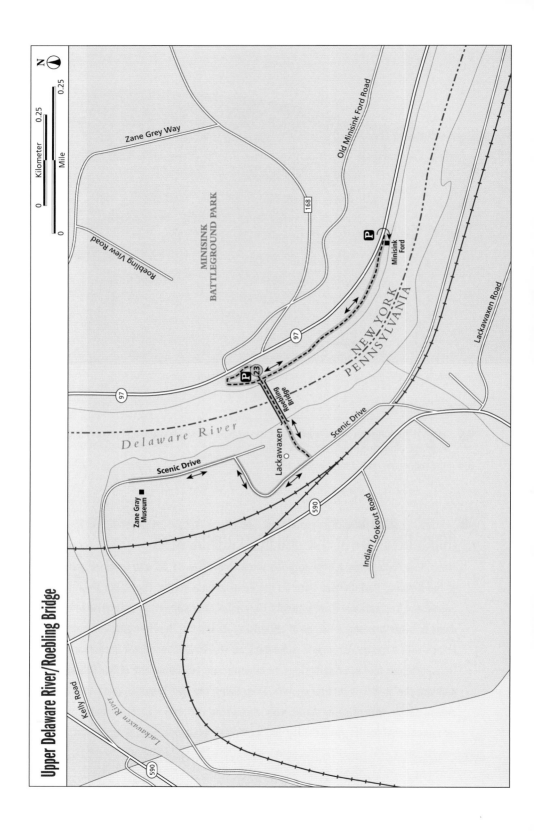

0.7 Reach the bridge; cross over into Pennsylvania for some additional views of the Upper Delaware River.

0.8 At the end of the bridge in Pennsylvania, bear right onto Scenic Drive. Follow the road around the bend to the right, and turn left on Scenic Drive to continue to the Zane Gray Museum. (**Note:** The museum's hours are limited; check to see if it will be open on the day of your visit.)

1.2 Reach the Zane Gray Museum. After your visit, return to the Roebling Bridge by the same route, and cross it to your car.

1.7 Arrive back at the parking area.

The Upper Delaware River flows along the New York–Pennsylvania border.

24 Minisink Battleground

This shady natural area once erupted in battle between British and American troops and the Mohawk Indians.

Start: Parking area at the Minisink Battle-ground Interpretive Center. The trail begins west of parking, on the park road (look for the gate).
Distance: 0.7-mile loop
Hiking time: About 45 minutes
Elevation gain: 151 feet
High point: 1,161 feet
Difficulty: Easy

Best season: Summer and fall
Traffic: Hikers only
Fees and permits: No fees or permits required
Maps: Available online at minisink.org/minisinkbattlemap.jpg
Trail contacts: Sullivan County Parks and Recreation, 100 North St., Monticello 12701; (845) 794-3000; co.sullivan.ny.us

Finding the trailhead: From NY 97 at the Roebling Bridge, head north on CR 168, following the signs to Minisink Battleground Park. The park entrance will be on your left. From the parking area, look west for the gate on the park road. This is the trailhead. GPS: N41 29.277' / W74 58.195'

The Hike

This little gem of a park is within the boundaries of the Upper Delaware Scenic and Recreational River, an area preserved by the National Park Service for its historic and natural value. Minisink Battleground is managed by Sullivan County, but like so many properties within national park boundaries that maintain their local oversight, it benefits from the park service's supervision as well as the involvement of passionate local professionals and volunteers.

Your walk along the Battleground Trail takes you through the story of a Revolutionary War battle with a cast of characters who may not be household names outside this local area—but who were critical to the fight for and against independence in southern New York. Here you will learn about the Mohawk Indians' loyalty to the British rather than the new Americans—unlike other tribes of the Iroquois Confederacy—and about the men who fought and died on both sides in the bloody battle. The last part of this hike passes through an area that supplied bluestone—a popular and highly valued paving and foundation stone—to much of the eastern United States in the early days of the new country.

We found something particularly delightful in this park: natural quiet, a commodity that has become hard to come by anywhere in the densely populated and well-traveled state of New York. Here you can hear yourself think, pick out the songs of various warblers and vireos in spring and early summer, and enjoy the rustling of leaves as squirrels, chipmunks, and robins make their way along the forest floor. While

Indian Rock honors the Iroquois who died at Minisink. ▶

Historical Background

With all that we know about the Revolutionary War and the lines of men in red coats facing lines of men in blue and homespun on the formal field of battle, another kind of battle receives less attention until we visit a place like Minisink Battleground. Here there were no regiments kneeling with muskets in uniform lines—instead, this battle came at the end of a long series of raids carried out on villages by mixed parties of Mohawk Indians and British soldiers led by Col. Joseph Brant.

A Mohawk warrior with a degree from Dartmouth College and a lifelong resident of this general area, Brant led the Indians who had thrown their lot in with the British Loyalists when the war began, believing that the outcome would favor the English and that their land would be returned to them once the conflict ended. Over the course of several days, Brant and his warring party tore through the Neversink Valley, torching buildings and farms, stealing cattle and horses, and leaving little for the families who populated the area.

The American militia came together quickly to retaliate and attempt to stop the marauders, forming two groups led by Lt. Col. Benjamin Tusten, a medical doctor, and Maj. Samuel Meeker from New Jersey. They moved up the river behind the Brant contingent, planning a surprise attack to recover the settlers' belongings and cattle rather than to make war. Soon a militia led by Col. John Hathorn joined the two bands on the move, bringing the total number of men at arms to roughly 120.

On July 22, 1779, the militias realized that Brant and his men were coming across the Delaware River at Lackawaxen, and they made ready to ambush the Mohawk and British. Moments before they would make their move, however, one of the Americans fired a shot—perhaps accidentally, perhaps on purpose—and alerted Brant to their location. In short order, Brant and his men moved to surround the militias on the hill that is now Minisink Battleground Park, cutting one militia off from the other two and causing panic among the Patriots. The remaining forty-five or fifty Americans attempted a rush up the hill to gain the high ground, forming a defensive square and battling valiantly to hold their own. Their strategy—or perhaps their lack of one—finally gave way, however, as Brant and his men scattered the square and killed the men who remained. By day's end, as many as fifty Americans had died in the battle, while only seven of Brant's men succumbed.

As you walk the well-groomed trail here, keep in mind that it's hard to pinpoint exactly where most of the battle took place, as there were no structures or earthworks constructed and only a handful of landmarks remain. The named rocks help give the battleground some definition: Sentinel Rock, from which Brant made his final attack through the defensive square; Hospital Rock, where Tusten and seventeen wounded men found themselves trapped; and Indian Rock, where legend has it that Brant buried his dead warriors (though no one has ever found evidence of this).

At Hospital Rock, an American doctor and 17 wounded soldiers lost their lives in an Iroquois and British attack.

Minisink Battleground

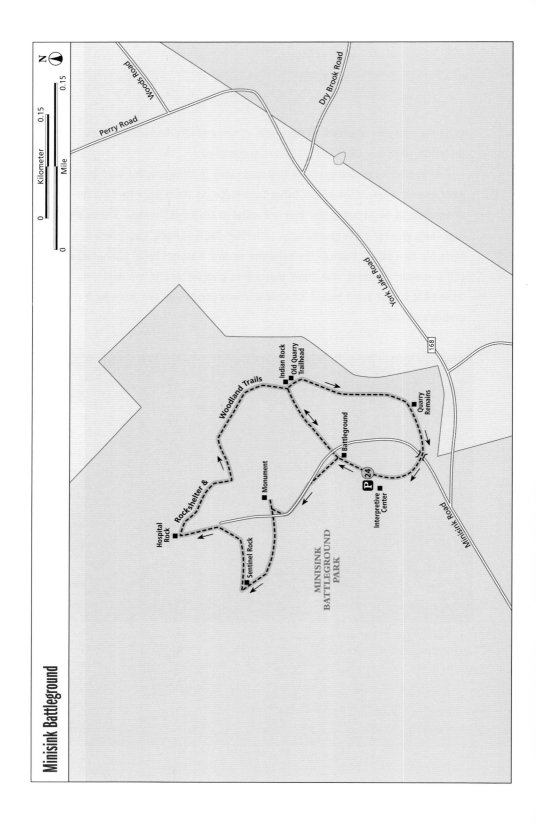

N

Kilometer
0   0.15   0.15

Mile
0

Woods Road

Perry Road

Dry Brook Road

York Level Road

168

Minisink Road

Woodland Trails

Indian Rock

Old Quarry Trailhead

Quarry Remains

Battleground

Hospital Rock

Rock shelter &

Monument

Sentinel Rock

P 24

Interpretive Center

MINISINK BATTLEGROUND PARK

the noise from NY 97 is only 1 mile or so away, the geography helps keep the traffic noise at bay so you can enjoy a bit of a wilderness experience in this little park.

Miles and Directions

0.0 Start at the gate on the park road, west of the parking area. Proceed past the gate and turn left onto the Battleground Trail.

0.1 At the top of the hill, follow the Battleground Trail to the left. There's a presentation area here with a monument dedicated in 1879 on the one-hundredth anniversary of the battle.

0.2 Come to Sentinel Rock, in the southwest corner of the square occupied by the American defense. This is the top of Rocky Hill. In another few feet, the Woodland Trail goes left. Continue straight.

0.3 Reach Hospital Rock, where Dr. Benjamin Tusten, who was a lieutenant colonel in the American army, gave medical attention to seventeen wounded soldiers. All these Americans were trapped and killed at this rock by British and Mohawk soldiers.

0.4 At the junction with the Rockshelter and Woodland Trails, continue straight on the Battleground Trail.

0.5 At Indian Rock, the Old Quarry Trail goes left. Turn left here to extend your walk. (**Option:** Continue straight for a quick return to the parking area.)

0.6 On the Old Quarry Trail, you can see sheer rock walls along the mossy dike. At the intersection, go right to return to the parking area.

0.7 Arrive back at the parking area.

25 Harriman State Park: Iron Mines Loop

Clear mountain lakes, forest-covered peaks, rocky outcroppings, and a summit with a spectacular view—it's all worth the extra effort Harriman demands.

Start: Off Seven Lakes Drive in the parking area for Lake Skannatati, 0.7 mile after the Kanawauke Circle
Distance: 2.7-mile loop
Hiking time: About 1.5 hours
Elevation gain: 1,001 feet
High point: 1,155 feet
Difficulty: More challenging
Best season: Apr through Nov

Traffic: Hikers only
Fees and permits: No fees or permits required
Maps: Available online at nynjtc.org/panel/goshopping
Trail contact: Palisades Interstate Park Commission, Bear Mountain 10911; (845) 786-2701; nysparks.us/parks/145/details.aspx
Special considerations: Boots with ankle support are a must in this park.

Finding the trailhead: From I-87 take exit 15A (Sloatsburg). Turn left at the bottom of the ramp onto NY 17 North and drive through Sloatsburg. Turn right at the first traffic light after the village onto Seven Lakes Drive. Continue on Seven Lakes Drive for 8 miles to the parking area for Lake Skannatati, on the left side of the road. (The parking area is 0.7 mile after the Kanawauke Circle.) GPS: N41 14.426' / W74 06.153'

The Hike

What does the quintessential downstate New York hike look like? Look no further than Harriman State Park, where this loop—a relatively easy hike compared to the legendary treks in the rest of the park—takes you through areas of mixed forest, huge boulders, and exposed faces of granite and metamorphic gneiss. The payoff comes at the top of Pine Swamp Mountain, a low peak by Adirondack standards but with a sweeping view of the surrounding Hudson Highlands. You'll be glad you braved the vigorous ascent when you arrive at the top.

The first part of this hike follows the Long Path, a footpath from Altamont in the Albany area all the way to the George Washington Bridge in Fort Lee, New Jersey. Originally a project of the Mohawk Valley Hiking Club, this 347-mile trail crosses the Shawangunk and Catskill Mountains, winding through salt marshes at its southern end and climbing to 4,000 feet in the Catskills' boreal forests. It's only recently that the "parakeet aqua" blaze color has been used from one end of the trail to the other, but wherever you see this shade, you'll know you're on the Long Path.

The rock-strewn trail through the former iron mining camp pays off in wide views of the park from the top.

Miles and Directions

0.0 Start following the aqua blazes at the northwest corner of the parking lot. You'll see white blazes with a red inverted triangle here as well; this is the trail on which you will return to the lot at the end of your hike. Almost immediately, another path goes right; bear left along the edge of the lake and follow the aqua blazes.

0.2 Turn right on the aqua-blazed path (the Long Path). Another path goes left here.

0.8 Cross a stream on large boulders. Begin a short ascent.

1.1 The yellow-blazed trail goes left and right here. Turn right on the yellow-blazed trail and begin following a dirt road.

1.5 Enter a young hemlock woods. The pond to your right is the center of Pine Swamp. Look for remnants of the Pine Swamp Mine ahead.

1.7 Reenter the woods here. Three yellow blazes on a tree signal the end of the yellow trail. Turn right and follow the white blazes with a red inverted triangle in the center. This is the Arden-Surebridge Trail (A-SB). Cross a stream on rocks (this may be a rushing cascade in spring). In about 10 steps there's a box canyon to your left. Explore if you wish, and continue on the A-SB when you're ready.

1.8 There's a cascade to your left; it may be dry in summer. In about 400 feet you'll see a remnant of a stone wall. This is all that remains of the area in which miners lived from the 1830s to the 1880s. The trail ascends steeply for a short stretch here and then begins an up-and-down section on a rockier path.

1.9 Begin a gradual but challenging 0.5-mile ascent to the top of Pine Swamp Mountain.

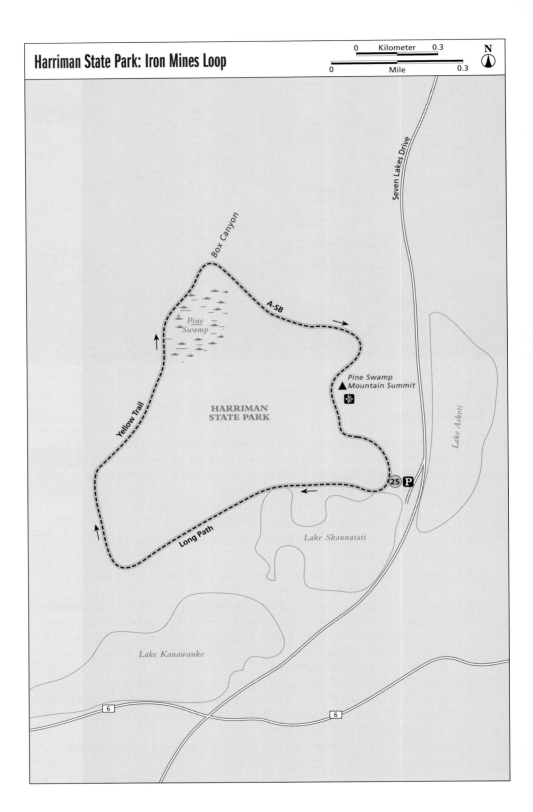

0   Kilometer   0.3

N

0   Mile   0.3

Seven Lakes Drive

Box Canyon

A-SB

Pine Swamp

Yellow Trail

Pine Swamp
Mountain Summit

HARRIMAN
STATE PARK

Lake Askoti

25   P

Long Path

Lake Skannatati

Lake Kanawauke

6

6

Historical Background

You may expect old-growth forest, but most of the trees here are second-growth, replanted after decades of iron mining stripped this area bare before and after the Civil War. The mines' furnaces required copious amounts of charcoal made from firewood, turning the forest into a continuous raw fuel source for iron ore processing. Mining stopped when Pennsylvania coal and Minnesota iron began to overshadow the Highlands' iron production at the turn of the twentieth century. That's when the Harriman family presented the State of New York with 30,000 acres of their private land adjacent to an existing park, turning this area into an outdoor paradise for hikers, campers, boaters, and many others.

While this hike takes you through the remains of some of these mines, they are not easy to spot, in part because the land has recovered so strongly from the mining days. Today the land appears as natural as it may have before the mines, the forests broken only by peaceful blue lakes and silver-gray rock faces jutting through the thriving understory.

2.4 Reach the summit of Pine Swamp Mountain at 1,165 feet. The view is obscured at this spot; continue to follow the trail to your left (south) for a better vantage point.

2.5 Here's the view you came to see. Lakes Skannatati and Askoti lie in front of you, and the forest-covered Catskill Mountains extend to the west, north, and south. You can see Seven Lakes Drive below, the only road that traverses this vista. When you're ready, follow the A-SB blazes downward to your left. The descent begins as a bit of a scramble over large boulders, but soon it becomes an easy, shady descent through the woods.

2.7 Arrive back at the parking area.

26 North-South Lake Campground Escarpment Trail Loop

There's no better way to take in the vibrant Catskill Mountains scenery than on this trail, where you will see the area from many angles.

Start: Parking area on Scutt Road in North-South Lake Campground
Distance: 4.9 miles for main loop; 7.2 miles total with three side trails
Hiking time: About 4 hours
Elevation gain: 509 feet
High point: 2,473 feet
Difficulty: Challenging
Best season: Spring through fall
Traffic: Hikers; cross-country skiers on some sections in winter
Fees and permits: Day-use fee at entrance for parking during peak seasons

Maps: Available online at catskillmountaineer .com/hiking-escarpment-SW.html
Trail contacts: North-South Lake Campground, CR 18, Haines Falls 12436; (518) 357-2289 or (518) 589-5058; www.dec.ny.gov/outdoor/ 24487.html
Special considerations: Black bears live in the Catskills, and they are frequently spotted in the vicinity of this trail. Before you undertake this hike, make sure you know what to do if you come across a bear in the woods. (See "Let's Talk about Bears" in this book's introduction.)

Finding the trailhead: From the south, take I-87 North to exit 20 at Saugerties. Follow NY 32 North for approximately 6 miles to NY 32A to NY 23A West. Stay on NY 23A to the village of Haines Falls. Take your first right onto CR 18. The campground entrance is at the end of the road in 2 miles.
From the north, take I-87 South to exit 21 at Catskill. Turn left onto NY 23 East and continue to NY 9W South. Follow NY 9W through Catskill to NY 23A. Follow 23A West to Haines Falls. Make the first right turn in Haines Falls onto CR18. The campground entrance is at the end of the road in 2 miles. GPS: N42 12.045' / W74 03.511'

The Hike

If you've heard about the Catskills but never visited, or if you've wondered about the best places to see the most sweeping views of the Catskill Mountains in their full glory—especially in fall—then this solid hiking experience is for you. Make a day of it, and explore all the side trails that lead to slices of the region's history in hospitality and tourism, and from which you can see the views that inspired the first truly American style and philosophy of fine art: the Hudson River School of landscape painting.

Your hike begins in the parking area at North-South Lake Campground, a stunningly beautiful area in its own right. From the parking area, walk up Scutt Road (it's easier and less annoying than the root-crossed blue-blazed trail at this point, though they both lead to the main trailhead), then follow the trail marked with blue DEC markers. Stay on the blue-blazed trail for most of this hike, leaving it to enhance your experience with side trails to magnificent Kaaterskill Falls, one of New York State's most dramatic waterfalls; and to the sites of the former Kaaterskill Hotel and Catskill Mountain House, two of the most popular mountain retreats for the wealthy when the Catskills provided a respite from the intense heat and foul air of a New York City summer.

Many of the landmarks that once dotted this land now remain only as foundations and memories, so Layman's Monument stands out as a place you may want to linger. This stone obelisk commemorates the courage of 25-year-old firefighter Frank Layman, who died here on August 10, 1900, when a forest fire engulfed him before he could jump off the ledge to escape. The monument stands where his comrades found him once the fire was under control, making this a particularly poignant place to pause as you walk this trail through the landscape he gave his life to save.

After the monument, a series of narrow ledges provide stunning views of the mountains, ravines, and valleys that make the Catskills such a popular place to hike. Watch your step as you traverse these slender overlooks; if you want to enjoy the view for a bit before you continue, stop walking while you do so.

When you're not faced with one wide, entrancing view of the area after another, your hike takes you through forested lands dominated by maple and oak trees, with some stands of paper birch and a scattering of conifers. The fragrant woods attract a wide variety of birds and small furry animals, as well as white-tailed deer and the occasional black bear. Keep your eyes and ears open for species you may not normally see in your own backyard, including the potential for deer, porcupine, and fisher, a weasel-like animal reintroduced in the Catskills in the early 1900s after hunters and trappers extirpated them. Some lucky hikers have the chance to spot a bobcat, an animal of minimal danger to humans (but bad news for rodents and birds).

Miles and Directions

0.0 Start from the Scutt Road parking area and walk south on Scutt Road.

0.4 Turn left and walk past the barrier.

0.5 At the trailhead, turn right. Follow the trail with blue trail markers. (**Option:** If you would like to explore a side trail right away, the other trail here takes you to Kaaterskill Falls, one of the tallest and most photographed falls in New York State. This trail only adds about 0.5 mile to your overall hike.)

0.6 Stop and register at the registry box. In a few minutes you will reach a major trail junction; go left on the Escarpment Trail.

1.2 Come to Layman's Monument. The trail turns left (east) here; continue to follow it.

1.3 Reach the first of several ledges (overlooks). This one provides a great view of Santa Cruz Falls and Buttermilk Ravine, where you may glimpse Buttermilk Falls.

1.4 This overlook provides more views of Buttermilk Falls and Buttermilk Ravine.

1.6 The yellow- and blue-blazed trails cross here. Continue straight on the Escarpment (blue) trail. (The yellow-blazed trail heads back to Scutt Road.)

1.7 At Sunset Ledge, you can look west toward Haines Falls and enjoy one of the iconic views of the Catskills.

Historical Background

North-South Lake Campground gets its name from two lakes that were once separated by a dam—one on land managed by Catskill Forest Preserve and one on private land. The original campground, developed here in the early 1930s, hugged the shoreline of North Lake and expanded as it became popular, with development of the beach in 1936. In the early 1970s the North Lake campground reached its current size, and some ten years later, South Lake became available for purchase. In 1984 the Department of Environmental Conservation (DEC) removed the strip of land between the two lakes, creating one large lake for the public's enjoyment.

Three major resorts served guests during "season" here from the mid-1800s into the mid-1900s: Kaaterskill Hotel, Laurel House, and the venerable Catskill Mountain House. These hotels drew the wealthiest city dwellers from all over the state and beyond, including a core group of artists of a uniquely American approach to painting known as the Hudson River School. Artists, including Thomas Cole, came to the Catskill Mountain House to paint the extraordinary view from its front lawn— Cole's famous *A View of the Two Lakes and Mountain House, Catskill Mountains, Morning* was one result of this activity. Authors Washington Irving, James Fenimore Cooper, and John Bartram all made reference to this resort in their writings, and three US presidents—Ulysses Grant, Chester Arthur, and Theodore Roosevelt—came here for a respite from the pressures of the office.

In 1880 a guest named George Harding asked a waiter if, instead of the usual beef the hotel's dining room served nightly, his daughter could have fried chicken because her doctor had sworn her off red meat. Charles Beach, Catskill Mountain House owner, refused so vociferously that the well-to-do Harding packed up his family and left, vowing to build his own rival hotel to put Beach out of business. The result was the Kaaterskill Hotel, constructed just a mile or so away, and it did indeed give the Mountain House a run for its money.

The Mountain House suffered a different blow, however, because of its claim that it stood on the highest peak in the Catskills, at 3,000 feet—even though its actual elevation was closer to 2,300 feet. In 1880 a geologist from Princeton University surveyed the Catskills and determined that the highest peak was actually Slide

Mountain, some distance southwest of Kaaterskill High Peak. This did not diminish the spectacle of the view from Catskill Mountain House, but it did signal the decline of the hotel's dominant position as the most popular resort in the area. The hotel continued to operate until it closed its doors in 1941. In 1963, in accordance with Catskill Forest Preserve policy, it was demolished in a controlled burn by the State of New York. (The Mountain House outlasted its rival, the Kaaterskill Hotel, by several decades. The Kaaterskill burned to the ground in an accidental fire in 1924.)

By contrast, the Laurel House began as a 50-room boardinghouse and grew to accommodate 300 guests, a fraction of the 1,200 rooms offered by the Kaaterskill Hotel. Laurel House attracted a middle-class traveler by charging roughly half the room-night fee asked by the two major resorts in the area. It offered the added bonus of a location just 100 feet from Kaaterskill Falls, where wooden steps helped guests climb down the falls to enjoy the view from its base. Like the Mountain House, Laurel House was destroyed in a state-sanctioned burn in 1967, leaving only its foundation standing in the forest to help us recall its history.

Artists of the Hudson River School selected a number of views to paint in the North-South Lake Campground.

North-South Lake Campground Escarpment Trail Loop

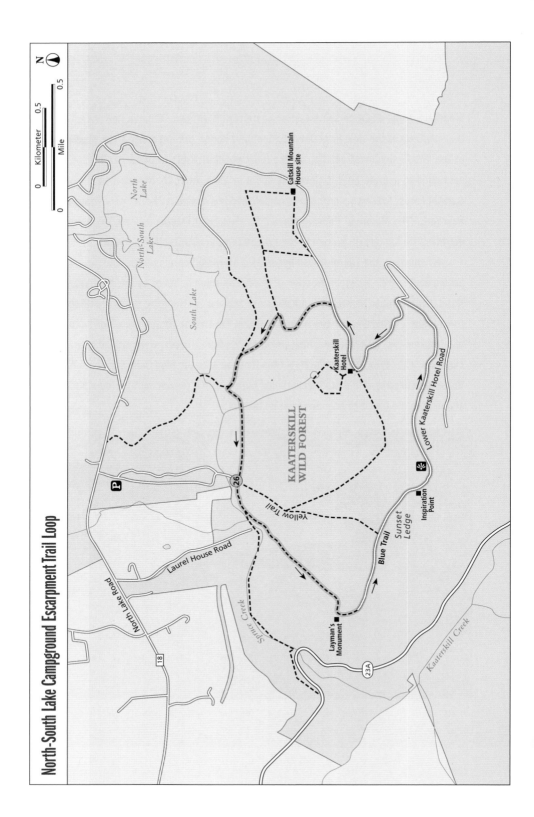

1.8 Inspiration Point offers an exceptional view of the edge of the Catskills and the valley beyond.

2.0 This overlook furnishes views of Poet's Ledge, Viola Ravine and Falls, Wildcat Ravine, Indian Head Ledge, and Buttermilk Ravine. The peaks in front of you are Kaaterskill High Peak and Round Top Mountain.

2.6 At the trail junction turn right on the Escarpment Trail. (The other trail will take you back to the parking area.) In less than 0.5 mile, another trail junction offers a route to Palenville Overlook and Palenville; bear left to stay on the Escarpment Trail loop.

3.0 At the junction with the trail to the Kaaterskill Hotel site, go straight for the short loop around the former hotel site or turn right on the Escarpment Trail.

3.3 Come to the junction with the trail to North-South Lake. Turn left to go to the lake, or keep going straight to visit Boulder Rock and the Catskill Mountain House site. This adds about 1.0 mile to your total hike but features some terrific views. When you're ready, continue left on this trail to North-South Lake. Watch your step on the Horseshoe Corner.

3.8 Reach North Lake Road and turn left on the road.

3.9 At the cross-country ski trail, turn left (off the road). Rejoin the main trail.

4.3 You're back at the beginning of the main trail. Turn right to return to your vehicle.

4.9 Arrive back at the parking area.

Take the side trail to see Kaaterskill Falls, one of the most photographed sights in the Catskills.

27 Onteora Lake / Bluestone Wild Forest

A small mountain lake serves as the centerpiece for this Catskills highlight, a former mining area now blanketed by fragrant forest.

Start: Trailhead kiosk in parking area at end of a gravel road off NY 28
Distance: 3.3-mile lollipop
Hiking time: About 1.75 hours
Elevation gain: 145 feet—repeatedly on this very hilly trail
High point: 540 feet
Difficulty: Moderate
Best season: Spring through fall

Traffic: Hikers only
Fees and permits: No fees or permits required
Maps: Available online at www.dec.ny.gov/lands/76293.html
Trail contact: New York Department of Environmental Conservation, 625 Broadway, Albany 12223; (516) 402-9405; e-mail: LF.Lands@dec.ny.gov

Finding the trailhead: From Kingston take NY 28 west for about 4 miles. Watch for the New York Department of Environmental Conservation (DEC) sign on your right just after the house at 904 NY 28 and just before the convenience store. Turn right onto the gravel road across from the sign and drive to the parking area. The kiosk marking the trailhead is easy to spot. GPS: N41 58.899' / W74 05.160'

The Hike

This fairly challenging hike looks deceptively simple at the outset. A well-maintained path leads to a satisfying view of Onteora Lake, with picnic tables and benches for your viewing and noshing enjoyment. Follow the trail into the woods, however, and you'll find plenty of ups and downs through the hills, peppered with dark rock faces that jut from the hillsides. You'll have ample opportunity to examine the bluestone for which this area is famous, as well as an impressive variety of fungi nestled between tree roots along the edges of the trail.

Wildlife abounds in this forest, so keep an eye open for eastern cottontails, gray and red squirrels, eastern chipmunks, white-tailed deer, and even a glimpse of a beaver. You'll see evidence of beaver activity along the lakeshore in the form of trunks gnawed down to cone-shaped points and poised to fall with the next big wind. Two large beaver houses stand in the lake, but the critters themselves are nocturnal, so chances are you'll only spot one if you happen to be hiking at dusk.

Use your ears to pick out the sounds of woodland warblers and vireos in spring and summer, as well as several species of woodpecker, white-breasted and red-breasted nuthatches, gray catbird, blue jay, northern cardinal, and many other year-round birds. Watch the ground for rustling leaves that can indicate wood and hermit thrushes,

You'll see evidence of beaver activity on the shores of Onteora Lake. ▶

Historical Background

What is bluestone, and why did it serve as a boom product in the mid-1800s? This bluish sandstone found throughout the Catskill Mountains was much in demand as a paving material because it stood up to the elements and offered an attractive slate-gray surface. Bluestone from the Catskills can be found in the base of the Statue of Liberty, in the Empire State Building, and in sidewalks and curbs throughout upstate New York and across the country.

This quarry outside Kingston sent the durable stone into the world on wagons pulled by teams of horses, bringing it to towns along the river for cutting and shaping to order. Stones ground and polished into curb and sidewalk blocks traveled up and down the river to the canals or to the ocean, moving swiftly (by nineteenth-century standards) to contractors across the country.

This all came to an abrupt end, however, with the development in 1880 of Portland cement. Made from limestone, shale, and other materials found in abundant supply across the country, the powdered cement product turned out to be so low-cost that it became immensely popular in a very short time. The bluestone mining operations soon went silent as Portland cement grew to dominate the paving and foundation construction market.

You can see the remains of bluestone mining operations as you follow this trail: Great slabs of fissured and chiseled rock punctuate the landscape among the hemlock, red maple, pine, and other trees that now cover the hillsides.

white-crowed and white-throated sparrows, and American robins in the warmer months.

Miles and Directions

0.0 Start walking north on the trail. Almost immediately you'll see a side trail to a picnic table at the lake. Stop to admire the lake then continue straight. The log-lined trail ends at the lake; just before that, a gravel trail goes left. Take the gravel trail.

0.3 Another trail joins from the left. Continue straight. The trail begins to climb through the woods.

0.5 Stop at the trail registry and register.

0.8 Watch for yellow markers at the beginning of the loop trail. Take the yellow-blazed trail.

Onteora Lake/Bluestone Wild Forest

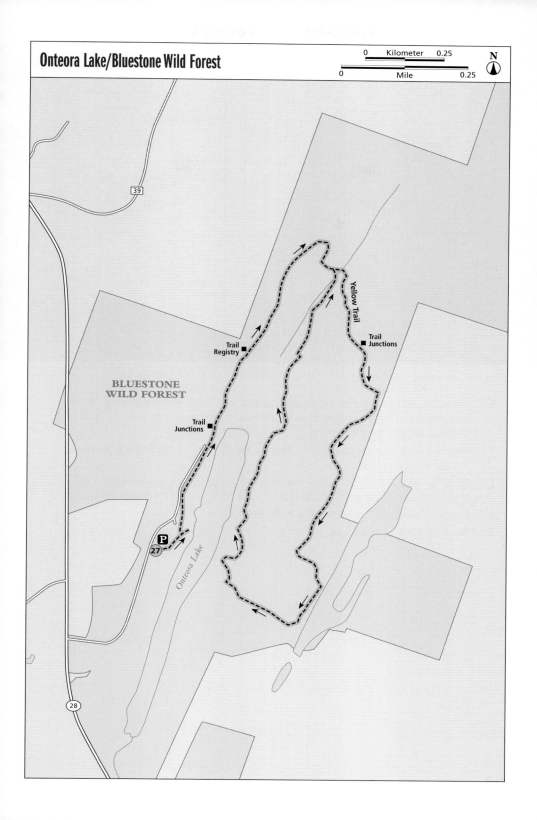

Exposed faces of bluestone are all that remain of the mining days near Onteora Lake.

1.0 The red-blazed trail begins to the left at a sign that says "Forest Preserve Parking." Continue straight on the yellow-blazed trail. On this stretch you can see sheared rock faces where bluestone mining took place.

1.1 The trail makes an emphatic right turn. Keep an eye out for some fascinating fungi through this damp, rocky stretch.

1.5 Reach the edge of the lake. The trail continues straight through the woods along the water then heads up into the woods with a water view. Watch for evidence of beaver activity.

2.5 Rejoin the main trail. Turn left to return to the parking area.

3.3 Arrive back at the parking area.

Central Leatherstocking Region

The shimmer of Otsego Lake gives Glimmerglass State Park its descriptive name.

28 Erie Canalway Trail: Warners to Camillus

This straight, shaded trail segment reaches the midpoint of the original Erie Canal at Sims' Store.

Start: Parking lot at Erie Canal Park in Warners
Distance: 4.2 miles out and back or 2.1-mile shuttle
Hiking time: About 1.5 hours for out-and-back hike; 1 hour or less for shuttle
Elevation gain: 104 feet
High point: 417 feet
Difficulty: Easy
Best season: Year-round

Traffic: Joggers, cyclists, cross-country skiers, snowmobilers in one section
Fees and permits: No fees or permits required
Maps: Trail map available online at nyscanals .gov
Trail contact: New York State Canal System, 200 Southern Blvd., Albany 12201; (800) 4CANAL4 (422-6254); nyscanals.gov

Finding the trailhead: From Syracuse take NY 173 West 9.8 miles to Warners. Erie Canal Park in Warners is at the corner of Newport Road and NY 173 (Warners Road). Park in the parking area off Newport Road. GPS: N43 04.551' / W76 19.623'

Shuttle drop-off: For a shuttle hike, leave a vehicle at Erie Canal Park in Camillus, 5750 Devoe Rd.; (315) 488-3409.

The Hike

From Albany to Buffalo, the Erie Canal towpath provides some of the most pleasant walking, biking, skating, and running trail footage in New York State, with about 380 miles of level, meticulously maintained pathways. This tiny segment of the total trail extends through Erie Canal Park northwest of Syracuse, ending in Camillus at the exact midpoint of the original canal and the 300-acre Erie Canal Park.

If you enjoy this short hike, consider a longer trek along the canal. The Old Erie Canal State Historic Park maintains 36 miles of the original canal and its modern trail from DeWitt to Rome, east of Syracuse, where paddlers, kayakers, equestrians, and snowmobilers join hikers for year-round outdoor recreation.

Miles and Directions

0.0 Start the hike on the stone-dust path along the canal. (*FYI:* There's a paved path into the park here; be sure to take the towpath on the edge of the canal.)

1.4 The trail becomes a shared road, with limited vehicular traffic. The road provides access only to the Camillus Sportsman's Club, so very few cars pass through here. The speed limit is 10 miles per hour.

Camillus Landing is the midpoint on the Erie Canalway.

Historical Background

This sample packs a great deal of canal history into its 2.1-mile stretch. A trace of the original Erie Canal, this was one of many sites that experienced significant improvements during the period of the Enlargement, from 1836 to 1862. Working to accommodate more and heavier barges—early barges weighed perhaps 30 tons, while boats carrying cargo in the early 1900s often weighed in at 3,000 tons—the Enlargement increased the canal's width from 40 to 70 feet, with a new depth of 7 feet instead of the 4 feet of water that had buoyed the lighter barges.

You'll actually walk on the towpath used by mules and oxen that towed barges along the canal, led by a "hoggee"—a boat driver, most often a boy in his teens. Today this canal segment is lined on either side by verdant foliage, with shade trees providing a sense of seclusion along the man-made waterway. The flat, easy walk ends at Camillus Erie Canal Park, where volunteers maintain a set of reproductions of buildings that stood here at the canal's halfway point in the 1800s. Plan to spend some time in the Sims' Store Museum, a carefully reproduced canal-side store circa 1860s that supplied merchants and barge drivers with medicine, food, water, and animal feed. Check the museum's current hours at townofcamillus.com.

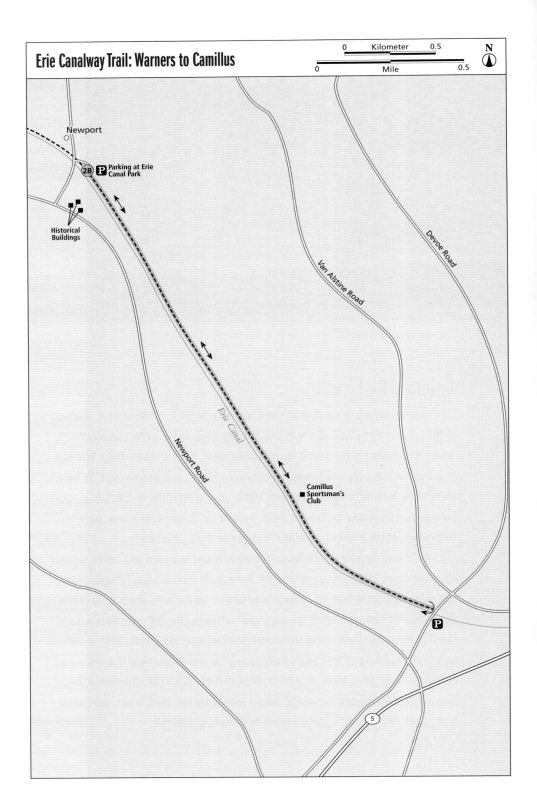

The Erie Canalway Trail offers a wide range of easy hikes.

2.1 Reach Erie Canal Park in Camillus; the historic building reproductions are on your left. The canal path continues from here to Waterford, New York, east of Albany. If you haven't arranged for a shuttle, turn back toward Warners and retrace your steps on the canal path.

4.2 Arrive back in Warners.

29 Fillmore Glen State Park

One waterfall after another tumbles through a narrow, lushly forested gorge, a place where the thirteenth president of the United States may have spent time in his youth.

Start: Parking area at the main pavilion
Distance: 2.4-mile loop
Hiking time: About 1.5 hours
Elevation gain: 525 feet
High point: 1,152 feet
Difficulty: Moderate
Best season: June through Oct
Traffic: Hikers only
Fees and permits: Entry fee per vehicle in season

Maps: Park map available online at parks.ny .gov/parks/attachments/FillmoreGlenTrailMap .pdf
Trail contact: Fillmore Glen State Park, 1686 NY 38, Moravia 13118; (315) 497-0139; parks.ny.gov/parks/157/details.aspx
Special considerations: If visiting in May, call the park to check the trail opening date. Watch for fallen, loose shale on the path.

Finding the trailhead: From Syracuse take NY 5 West about 22 miles to the junction with NY 38 in Auburn. Turn south onto NY 38 and continue 17 miles to the park entrance in Moravia. Park at the main pavilion; the trailhead is behind the building and up the paved path. GPS: N42 41.932' / W76 24.981'

The Hike

If you're only going to take one hike in central New York, make it Fillmore Glen. Rarely do we find such a magical combination of striking geological formations, glistening gorge walls that weep with spring runoff, a storybook forest, and no fewer than five waterfalls—including one that plummets from a creek tributary at the top of the gorge. Tie all of this with an ingenious system of eight bridges that cross and recross the gorge, laced together by a pathway reinforced with natural stone guard walls, and you have the kind of hiking experience for which the Finger Lakes region is famous.

It's no surprise that glaciers played the initial role in shaping the gorge as the rush of glacial meltwater tore through the area and slashed through the surface shale to the limestone bedrock below. Today the surrounding shale continues to erode—you're likely to see recent crumbles as you hike—but the tenacious vegetation plays a role in holding much of it in place, covering the jagged rock faces with mosses, lichens, and vines.

While this hike is fairly easy in dry weather, the gorge creates a microclimate in which the humidity remains high. Stone steps and earthen pathways can be slippery, and water often drips (or cascades) from the porous shale walls, especially after a heavy rain. Two pieces of advice on this:

Historical Background

Chances are, you don't often think about the thirteenth president of the United States, so it may not occur to you that this park is actually named for him. Millard Fillmore was born in this area, just outside Moravia, and the park contains a replica of the cabin in which he was born. You'll find it as you proceed to the main pavilion to begin your hike; it's on the south side of the parking area. Fillmore lived in such a log cabin with his parents and eight brothers and sisters, growing up in a farming community and attending a one-room school until he was 15, when his father apprenticed him to a cloth maker in Sparta, New York, some distance west of here on the other side of the Finger Lakes region. The White House website notes: "Millard Fillmore demonstrated that through methodical industry and some competence, an uninspiring man could make the American dream come true." Perhaps this is not the way a US president hopes to be remembered, but history considers this an accurate statement.

(1) Wear footwear that will grip in wet conditions.

(2) Don't miss the hanging gardens of ferns and clinging vines that result from the constant seeps through the multilayered shale.

Miles and Directions

0.0 Start at the trailhead behind the pavilion and head up the paved path.

0.1 The swimming area is to the left of the path, created by one of two dams in Dry Creek. Keep right and continue on the paved path.

0.2 Turn right onto the Gorge Trail. (Don't cross the bridge here; that's the route to the North Rim.) Take the stairway to the right; it's 140 steps to the top. (**Option:** Park in the lot at the top of the stairs to save yourself the fairly aerobic climb.) At the top of the steps turn left on the Gorge Trail.

0.3 Reach the overlook for Cowsheds Falls. Turn right and continue to the first of eight bridges.

0.4 Cross Bridge 1 and enter the dense, sultry forest. Stop here a moment to notice the fascinating patterns of moss on the trees and the change in the light quality as the sun works to filter through the leafy canopy. On the other side of this patch of forest, cross Bridge 2.

0.5 Cross Bridge 3.

0.6 Cross Bridge 4 and begin a steady incline.

0.7 Reach the top of the incline and a small waterfall.

0.8 Cross a series of platforms over runoff streams.

0.9 Cross Bridges 5 and 6.

1.0 A tributary creek originating at the top of the gorge sends a spectacular waterfall down through the glen wall. As you continue on the trail, don't miss the hanging gardens created by the seeps through the stacked shale walls.

1.1 Cross Bridge 7 and go up a staircase of about thirty steps.

1.2 Walk down sixteen steps to a falls overlook. When you're ready, walk up sixteen steps on the other side of the overlook and continue on the trail.

1.3 Come to Bridge 8, the last bridge on the Gorge Trail. The South Rim Trail crosses the bridge. To complete the Gorge Trail, do not cross this bridge; continue straight. To follow the North Rim Trail to make a loop, as described here, continue straight as well. In about 200 feet the Gorge Trail ends. (**Option:** Return to the trailhead by retracing your steps on the Gorge Trail.) To continue the loop, climb to the North Rim using the switchbacks ahead. (*FYI:* The climb to the North Rim involves a 150-foot elevation change.)

1.4 At the top of the gorge, turn left on the North Rim Trail. Cross a little bridge over a feeder stream.

Well-maintained trails, bridges and waterfalls are highlights at Fillmore Glen.

Fillmore Glen State Park

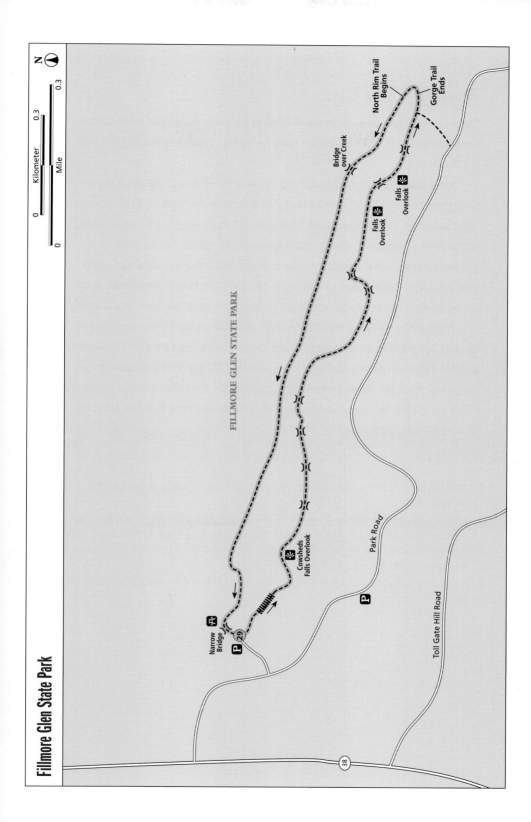

FILLMORE GLEN STATE PARK

Narrow Bridge

Cowsheds Falls Overlook

Falls Overlook

Falls Overlook

Bridge over Creek

North Rim Trail Begins

Gorge Trail Ends

Park Road

Toll Gate Hill Road

N

Kilometer
0   0.3

Mile
0   0.3

Roosevelt's "Tree Army"

We owe a debt of gratitude to President Franklin Delano Roosevelt and to the Civilian Conservation Corps (CCC) for the five years its workers devoted to building this trail in Fillmore Glen.

Nicknamed "Roosevelt's Tree Army" because of the billions of trees they planted throughout the United States, more than 2 million young men ages 17 to 25 learned skills including reforestation, forest protection and improvement, soil conservation, recreational development, range rehabilitation, aid to wildlife, flood control, drainage, reclamation, and emergency rescue activities. Each of these unmarried, otherwise unemployed men served six months to two years, working in the nation's state and national parks and on other municipal projects throughout the Great Depression.

Here in Fillmore Glen from 1934 to 1938, CCC workers lived in barracks right in the park and performed a wide range of services that made this park one of the most delightful places in central New York. The men of the CCC improved and extended the gorge trail, built the sturdy stone bridges, constructed the bathhouse and storage buildings, graded the campgrounds and playing fields, and even built the dam that created the swimming area.

1.7 Reach the source of the large waterfall you saw in the gorge. Cross a bridge over this tributary creek.

2.3 After a gentle descent on stone steps, bear left on the fork in the trail and proceed down a series of steps defined by railroad ties, followed by more stone steps. At the bottom, you've reached Dry Creek and the picnic area on the north side of the gorge. Bear right and cross the parking lot to your left.

2.4 Cross the creek using the narrow bridge over the spillway and arrive back at the parking lot.

30 Glimmerglass State Park and Hyde Hall

A cursed mansion, a sparkling lake, and a covered bridge—you'll find all of these in this jewel of a park.

Start: Sleeping Lion Trailhead, in the parking area at Hyde Hall in Glimmerglass State Park
Distance: 2.5-mile loop
Hiking time: About 1.5 hours
Elevation gain: 484 feet
High point: 1,656 feet
Difficulty: Moderate
Best season: Summer and fall

Traffic: Hikers only
Fees and permits: Entrance fee in some seasons
Maps: Trail map available at nysparks.com/parks/attachments/GlimmerglassTrailMap.pdf
Trail contacts: Glimmerglass State Park, 1527 CR 31, Cooperstown 13326; (607) 547-8662; nysparks.com/parks/28/details.aspx

Finding the trailhead: From I-90 (New York State Thruway), take exit 30 to Herkimer. Follow NY 28 South for about 12 miles to US 20. Turn left (east) onto US 20, and continue 11 miles to CR 31 south. Turn right onto CR 31 and watch for the entrance to Glimmerglass State Park on your right. In the park, drive straight to the parking area on Otsego Lake, in front of Hyde Hall. The trailhead is at the west end of the parking area. GPS: N42 47.540' / W74 52.531'

The Hike

Glimmerglass State Park has a great deal to recommend it—from a historic covered bridge to an estate that holds what was once the largest mansion in America—but neither of these things are easily seen from the Sleeping Lion Trail. You will pass the covered bridge as you drive into the park from the entrance; watch for it on your right (signs will point you in its direction). You can drive up to the bridge and park if you'd like to get a closer look, and a trail takes you through the bridge and loops through another pleasant section of the park.

Sleeping Lion Trail does explore the grounds of the former estate of George Hyde Clarke and his family, and you can imagine them hiking, hunting, and enjoying the views from this land as you complete the loop. You may want to check the tour schedule at Hyde Hall and plan your hike around a chance to see the inside of this eighteenth-century mansion.

The trail leads around and to the summit of Mount Wellington, with some heart-pumping slopes that climb upward for a change in elevation of nearly 500 feet, so be prepared for some solid cardio activity. While the trail has plenty of appeal as a route through a fragrant and sun-dappled forest, its eventual summit does not provide the hoped-for views of Otsego Lake and the surrounding countryside. Hike this one for the pleasure of being outdoors; then relax with the panoramic lake view at the end of the hike as you follow the road past Hyde Hall to your vehicle.

Historical Background

Two significant historic sites grace this park. The first, Hyde Hall Covered Bridge, is the oldest existing covered bridge in the United States, providing a 53-foot crossing over Shadow Brook. Built in 1823, this bridge features Burr Arch truss construction, which bears the entire load of the bridge while the kingpost truss keeps the bridge rigid. Other covered bridges were built as much as one hundred years or more before this one, but they all have succumbed to centuries of wind and weather, while this one has withstood the elements.

The fifty-room neoclassical mansion you will see on your way to the trailhead is Hyde Hall, the largest single-family home in America at the time of its construction. Landowner George Hyde Clarke supervised the design and building of this sprawling home, encouraged by his wife, Anne Low Cary Cooper, to make it ever larger and more impressive than any other in the area.

Clarke was the grandson of a man of the same name, an Englishman who bought up more than 120,000 acres of land in the Hudson and Mohawk Valleys during his tenure as governor of New York under the British Crown. After the Revolutionary War, when many of the English vacated their land in the new United States, young George Hyde Clarke came here to claim his fortune. But ownership of his land was now a point of contention among tenants who had farmed the land for generations. Clarke took his case to court, beginning with the New York circuit courts and working his way all the way up to the Supreme Court of the United States. There, in the sixth year of his legal woes over his grandfather's holdings, he won his case.

Clarke had imagined his mansion for nearly a decade before he could finally begin the project. He married Ann Low Cary Cooper, a recent widow who seemed to

White-tailed deer, chipmunks, squirrels, and perhaps groundhogs or raccoons may show themselves during your hike, and birds abound to feed on natural seeds and insects aplenty in this healthy forest.

The hike begins and ends at Hyde Bay on Otsego Lake, the one author James Fenimore Cooper named "Glimmerglass" in his eighteenth-century Leatherstocking Tales series of novels. On a calm day when the lake shimmers in the sunlight, you can see exactly why Cooper applied this moniker, and why it has stuck since the mid-1700s. Fishing, swimming, boating, paddling, and exploring the beach are all the surrounding neighbors to be a little too soon remarried. They even suggested that Ann's relationship with George may have begun before her husband, Richard Cooper, took leave of this earth. No one could deny her right to remarry, however, and soon Ann was well established on the Hyde estate, sharing her new husband's enthusiasm and vision for the mansion they would inhabit together. For seventeen years, George oversaw the construction of one wing after another, finally finishing the magnificent built estate in 1834 . . . and then he died in 1835, barely a year after seeing his favorite project through to completion.

Legend has it that George and Ann's son, also named George Hyde Clarke, ordered his mother out of the house when he turned 21. She turned around and cursed the house and any woman who would live in it. This tale only appears in one source, however—a book of stories about the region collected by James Fenimore Cooper II, descendent of the vaunted author of the same name who wrote more than 150 years earlier. Cooper II recorded the stories passed down verbally by his family, one of which involved Ann's curse on her former home. The curse didn't carry much weight with the fates, however; women who lived in Hyde Hall apparently fared quite well for several generations, until the upkeep of such an expansive property became too much for the remainder of the Clarke fortune to support. In 1964 the Friends of Hyde Hall formed to preserve the estate and save the mansion from demolition, quickly applying for and achieving registry on the National Register of Historic Places. Today the same organization, now known as Hyde Hall, Inc., maintains the mansion and tends to its continuing restoration.

encouraged here; you may want to make a day of it with lunch at one of the park's many picnic tables and a dip in the waters. This is one of New York's prettiest parks, so leave yourself time to enjoy it to the fullest.

Miles and Directions

0.0 Start at the west end of the parking area. Otsego Lake is to the south and west, and Hyde Hall is to the north. The path to the Sleeping Lion Trailhead begins as mowed grass and quickly changes to a dirt road. Stop and sign in at the registry before proceeding.

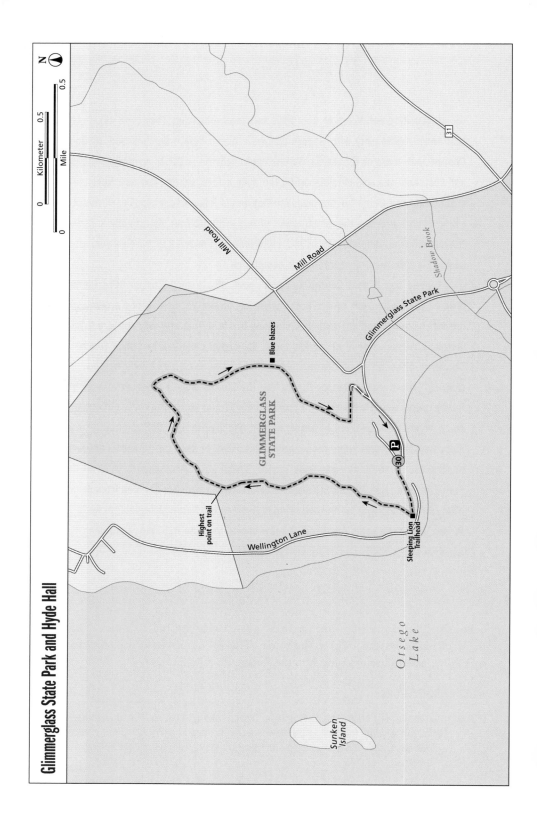

Glimmerglass State Park and Hyde Hall

N

Kilometer
0   0.5

Mile
0   0.5

Mill Road

Mill Road

31

Shadow Brook

Glimmerglass State Park

Blue blazes

GLIMMERGLASS
STATE PARK

P
30

Highest
point on trail

Wellington Lane

Sleeping Lion
Trailhead

Otsego
Lake

Sunken
Island

In the early 19th century, Hyde Hall was the largest home in the United States.

0.2 Turn right onto the Sleeping Lion Trail. Follow the red blazes for now; the blaze colors change frequently on this trail.

0.8 Here the red trail blazes are joined by orange ones. You will continue to see orange blazes throughout this hike, with additional colors to signal changes. Here it's all uphill; the trail gets steep for a stretch.

1.7 The trail levels off as it curves west.

2.1 As you begin to descend, blue blazes appear along with the orange.

2.4 Reach a gravel road. Turn left and take it to the paved road; turn right onto the pavement and continue to the parking area.

2.5 Complete the loop and arrive back at the parking area.

Rochester

High Falls provided the power for grain mills in the nineteenth century—giving Rochester its original nickname, the "Flour City."

31 Genesee Riverway Trail and Rochester Lighthouse

This award-winning boardwalk trail descends quickly from the park to the Genesee River, crossing the river's turning basin on a gently winding elevated walkway.

Start: Parking area in Turning Point Park, at the end of Boxart Street in Charlotte
Distance: 4.4 miles out and back
Hiking time: About 2.25 hours
Elevation gain: 143 feet
High point: 325 feet
Difficulty: Moderate
Best season: Spring through fall

Traffic: Cyclists, in-line skaters, cross-country skiers
Fees and permits: No fees or permits required
Maps: Available at cityofrochester.gov/grt
Trail contact: City of Rochester Recreation Bureau, 400 Dewey Avenue, Rochester 14613; (585) 428-6755; www.cityofrochester.gov/grt

Finding the trailhead: From I-590 North, take the NY 104 West exit. Continue on NY 104 West to Lake Avenue and turn right onto Lake. Take Lake Avenue to Boxart Street and turn right. Follow Boxart Street around a sharp left turn at the International Paper plant; continue on Boxart to the end at the Turning Point Park parking lot. The trailhead is on the east side of the parking lot, overlooking the Genesee River. GPS: N43 13.646' / W77 37.074'

The Hike

I've chosen the northernmost section of the 16-mile Genesee Riverway Trail because of its many attributes: It's easily accessed with plenty of parking, this part of the trail does not require any walking on city roads, and it follows the river gorge from the

The Lighthouse at the Mouth of the Genesee

The Charlotte-Genesee Lighthouse stands in its original spot—but it was much closer to Lake Ontario when it was built. When the city built the piers to prevent sandbars from forming across the mouth of the river, the natural deposits of sand created a beach that extended farther out into the lake each year. The lighthouse was deactivated in the early 1880s, but a recent renovation of the lantern room allowed the local lighthouse historical society to put the light back on the US Coast Guard's "active" list, making it the oldest active surviving lighthouse on Lake Ontario. It's just forty-two steps and an eleven-rung ladder to the lantern room, if you're thinking of making a side trip to climb the lighthouse.

Historical Background

It's hard for us to imagine now that back in 1806, the settlement of Charlotte served as one of the principal ports on Lake Ontario, the stopping place for boats stocked with wheat, pork, potash, and whiskey between Oswego to the east and Lewiston to the west. The mouth of the Genesee River created a navigable and easily accessible route to the upstate cities just south of the lake, much more so than Irondequoit Bay, where a sandbar at the bay's mouth created a hazard for the small sailing vessels of the time. At the time Charlotte was little more than a handful of shacks and log houses. But no settlement existed yet at what would become Rochester, so the town at the mouth of the river became a place to trade for goods that would fetch top dollar once buyers at the next port heard they were from the Genesee area.

When the War of 1812 arrived, Charlotte's position at the river's mouth made it a target of conflict, so settlers established a new trading post 3 miles up the river in 1817. Carthage had a dock and a wooden arch bridge across the Genesee River Gorge, but the bridge collapsed in 1820, dashing hopes of making Carthage the primary port on the river. Focus shifted back to the river's mouth as the war ended, and the transport of goods all the way to the Upper Falls made it possible to establish a mill town there. Rochester was born in 1812, growing rapidly as its mills turned grain into flour (hence the nickname "Flour City") and logs into lumber for shipment to parts west and to Canada. Large schooners and powered ships made their way up the river to Rochester, including the 110-foot-long *Ontario*, the first steamboat to arrive in the Genesee River, followed a few years later by the *Martha Ogden*.

It wasn't long, however, before the Erie Canal made it easier to transport goods and materials along the upstate New York corridor from the Hudson and Mohawk

Rivers all the way to Lake Erie; and the arrival of railroads in the late 1830s drew trade away from the Port of Rochester and toward the inland routes across the state. The federal government had provided significant funds for improvements at the port in the 1820s, however, including construction of the two piers and lighthouses—the Charlotte-Genesee Lighthouse and another one at the northern end of the western pier—so attempts to draw more commerce to the lake port continued for decades. Steamboats transported passengers along the south shore, maintaining a daily schedule from Ogdensburg to Lewiston, and a Canadian firm sent its own passenger boats across the lake between Hamilton and Toronto, Ontario, and Rochester and Kingston, New York.

In the 1870s and 1880s, a coal trestle brought coal down from railroad cars to large ships in the turning basin so that they could take this coal across the lake to Canada. This became a major export for the Port of Rochester, weighing in at 350,000 tons of cargo or more, while all other exports combined achieved a weight of less than 20,000 tons. Even this industrial use faded over time as other energy sources gained stature, and the port eventually became a recreation center, with spurts of activity around the paper pulpwood trade and other natural resources in the 1920s. By the mid-twentieth century, however, the import-export trade had declined enough that the city had begun to look at alternative uses for the Port of Rochester, the Genesee River, and the turning basin. The walkway you see today is a twenty-first-century improvement that not only repurposes this part of the river for the public enjoyment but also acknowledges the end of the shipping era in favor of trucking and railroads that transport raw materials more rapidly and cost-effectively.

The Genesee Riverway Trail leads through the river's historic Turning Basin.

turning point from which the park gets its name. It also provides a slice of history with which even lifelong residents of Rochester may not be truly familiar.

You'll begin at Turning Point Park, a 275-acre gem loaded with hiking and biking trails of its own. From the parking lot, walk down the paved trail to the 3,572-foot-long elevated walkway that leads through the Genesee River Turning Basin. Beyond the turning basin, the trail extends into the busy marina area just south of the Port of Rochester. You'll pass the 1822 Charlotte-Genesee Lighthouse, which is open to visitors from early May through the end of October.

When you reach the Port of Rochester building, you may wish to continue walking to view Ontario Beach straight ahead before returning through the basin.

Miles and Directions

0.0 Start at the information kiosk on the east side of the parking lot; you can see the paved trail making a long descent from here to the river. Follow the curving trail around the side of the gorge for about 0.3 mile, until you're level with the river.

0.3 At the bottom of the hill, you've reached the river basin. The signpost directs you either right to Lake Avenue and the City of Rochester or left to the Port of Rochester. Turn left.

0.5 You're on a raised walkway that crosses the turning basin, where large ships can turn around after entering from Lake Ontario. As you walk along here, you'll come to Red Falls— look for the falling water directly below the cellular tower.

1.0 The raised walkway over the basin ends and you begin a gentle ascent to street level on a paved pathway.

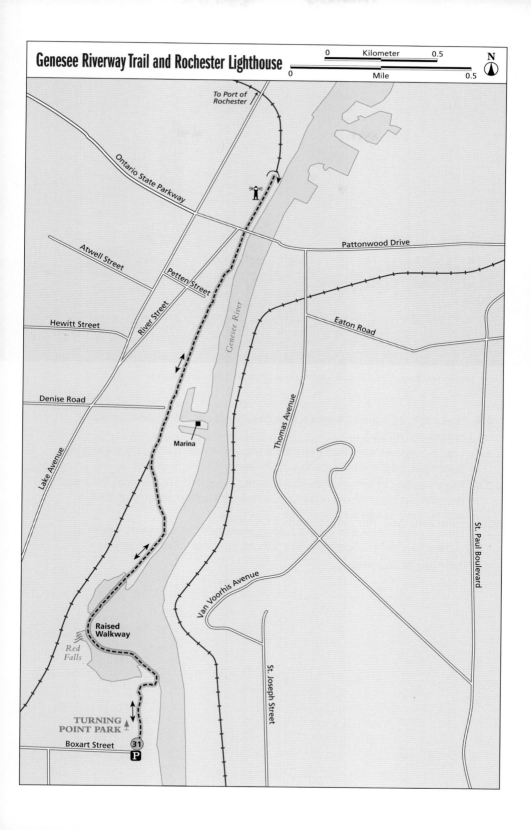

Genesee Riverway Trail and Rochester Lighthouse

0 Kilometer 0.5

0 Mile 0.5

N

To Port of Rochester

Ontario State Parkway

Atwell Street

Petten Street

Pattonwood Drive

Hewitt Street

River Street

Eaton Road

Denise Road

Genesee River

Lake Avenue

Marina

Thomas Avenue

St. Paul Boulevard

Van Voorhis Avenue

Raised Walkway

Red Falls

St. Joseph Street

TURNING POINT PARK

Boxart Street

31

P

From the end of the pier at Ontario Beach State Park, weather can hammer the modern lighthouse.

1.3 To your right, a commercial marina is crowded with sailboats and motorboats in spring, summer, and early fall.

1.7 Cross Petten Street and continue on the trail through the three posts on the opposite side of the street. The paved trail goes on along the river, paralleling River Street.

2.0 Reach a parking lot and one of the official starting points for the Riverway Trail. The original Rochester Lighthouse is on your left. Continue straight along the path through this busy waterfront area to the Port of Rochester.

2.2 Reach the Port of Rochester Terminal building, where you'll find restaurants, a snack bar, and restroom facilities. Stop here before retracing your steps to Turning Point Park.

4.4 Arrive back at the parking lot.

32 Erie Canalway Trail: Pittsford to Fairport

This historic canal towpath is now an 84-mile recreational trail, a developed stretch of the canal's total 360 miles. This section reveals the canal's famous Great Embankment, meanders through three charming towns, and offers food, drink, and services at each end and at its midpoint.

Start: On the Erie Canal path across from 45 Schoen Place in the town of Pittsford
Distance: 6.0-mile shuttle
Hiking time: About 3 hours
Elevation gain: 102 feet
High point: 501 feet
Difficulty: Moderate
Best season: Apr through Nov

Traffic: Cyclists, in-line skaters in paved areas, cross-country skiers
Fees and permits: No fees or permits required
Maps: Canalway map and guide available at eriecanalway.org/documents/ECNHC_Map Guide_2012_web.pdf
Trail contact: New York State Canal Corporation, 200 Southern Blvd., Albany 12201; (518) 436-2700; www.nyscanals.gov

Finding the trailhead: From I-590 North or South, take the Monroe Avenue/Pittsford exit and turn east onto Monroe Avenue (NY 31). Drive 2.5 miles through Brighton and Pittsford to the Village of Pittsford. Turn left onto NY 96 (North Main Street), cross the Erie Canal, and take the next right onto Schoen Place. Drive through Schoen Place to the Bella Amore pottery shop on your left at 45 Schoen Pl., and turn left after the building, driving down the slope into the parking lot. The hike begins at the gazebo across the road from Bella Amore, alongside the canal. GPS: N43 05.398' / W77 30.669'

Shuttle drop-off: In Fairport take I-490 east to exit 25 for Fairport/NY 31F. Turn left at the end of the ramp and drive 2.5 miles to O'Connor Road. Turn left and drive to the second parking lot. The canal path is in front of you, along the north side of the canal. GPS: N43 06.111' / W77 27.350'

The Hike

We won't actually travel "15 miles on the Erie Canal"—we'll stop at 6, enough for a satisfying walk along the water on a fine spring day or a crisp fall afternoon. In the canal's heyday, mules walked this towpath to propel barges up and down the water's length, and you'll gain some appreciation for their labors as you stride along this historic, enduringly appealing pathway.

Today this peaceful canal transports little more than pleasure crafts and tour boats, but its place in history is sealed. And thanks to the foresight of organizations including the New York State Canal Corporation and the Erie Canalway National Heritage Corridor, the Erie Canal Heritage Trail is one of the most popular pathways from Albany to Buffalo.

You'll pass through three canal town centers on this hike—Pittsford, Bushnell's Basin (actually a hamlet of Perinton), and Fairport—while walking straight across

Erie Canalway offers a well-groomed trail along the canal's original towpath.

Perinton to reach Fairport from Pittsford. All three of these towns offer shopping and dining experiences right on the canal, from the boutiques and gift emporia of Schoen Place to the quirky shops in Fairport's Packett's Landing.

And here's the most important note of all: In each town you'll find one of Rochester's premier ice cream confectioners, all of which make their own confections. In Pittsford make a stop at the family-owned Pittsford Farms Dairy and Bakery at 44 N. Main St., just before you enter Schoen Place, where the rich and delicious ice cream is made right on the premises—and you can pick up some just-baked cookies for your hike. Bushnell's Basin features the world-famous Abbott's Frozen Custard, a creamier concoction than ice cream. They've been perfecting their astonishing chocolate almond custard since 1902, so be sure to stop for a taste. In Fairport the Moonlight Creamery offers all-natural "artisan" ice cream in rich flavors like Second Date, Inauguration Day, and Maui Wowie, along with shade-grown coffee and handmade chocolates. After walking 6 miles, you'll deserve a treat!

Miles and Directions

0.0 Start the hike at the gazebo in front of Bella Amore. Walk east (to your left as you face the canal) under the trestle bridge.

0.6 A trestle bridge for NY 31 passes overhead. Continue straight along the canal.

Historical Background

The Erie Canal, built from 1817 to 1825, began as the brainchild of Governor DeWitt Clinton, whose passionate involvement in the project earned the canal the nickname "Clinton's Ditch." Those who scoffed at the fabulously expensive undertaking soon saw the sense in Clinton's vision, however, as the canal became an engineering marvel and one of the crowning American achievements of the nineteenth century. The canal not only created an open lane of commerce across the state and into the new western territories but also put thousands of immigrants—most of them Irish—to work for nearly a decade as they dug trenches, reinforced them with cement, and created the locks that raise and lower barges through the hills of upstate New York.

From Albany to Buffalo, the original 363-mile Erie Canal transformed the way business was done throughout New York State. Farmers, mining and lumber companies, and manufacturers now had a way to transport goods and materials that came up the Hudson River from New York City into upstate New York and on to Lake Erie, where these shipments could reach into the western frontier. At the same time, the canal brought crops, goods, and materials from the Midwest to the Northeast, as barges loaded with grain and natural resources traveled from Illinois, Wisconsin, Minnesota, Ohio, Michigan, and points west to mills and ports in New York.

With merchandise traveling at many times the speed of a horse and wagon, New York State became the main conduit to waterways including the St. Lawrence Seaway, the Hudson River, and Lake Champlain, carrying materials up into New England and bringing iron ore, lumber, granite, bluestone, garnets, and much more out of the northeastern states. Settlements to the west grew and prospered, opening new territories to construction and enterprise. In New York, port cities including Buffalo, Rochester, Syracuse, Albany, and New York City became the busiest and most populated cities in America.

0.9 A connector trail goes down to the left into a Pittsford neighborhood. To your right you can see the first of two floodgates you'll pass on this hike. Floodgates are a precaution in the event that a canal wall breaks, to keep the water from flooding the surrounding neighborhood.

1.1 Another neighborhood connector trail begins here to your left. Continue straight.

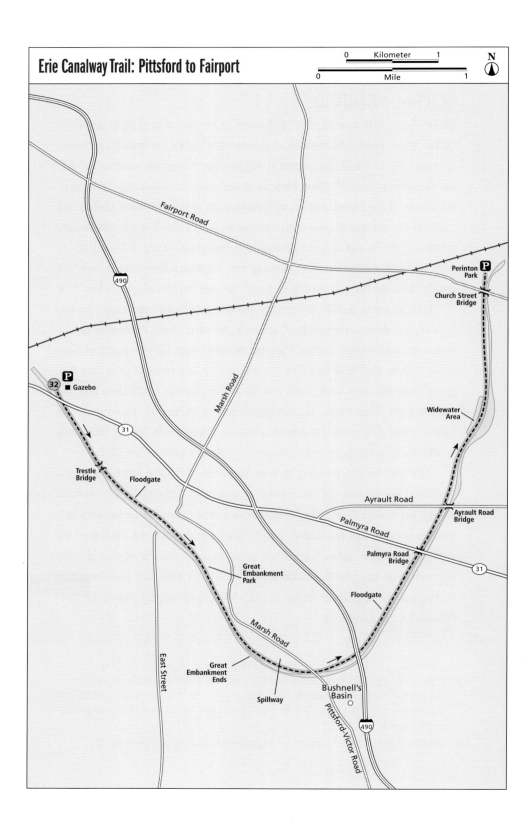

Erie Canalway Trail: Pittsford to Fairport

N

0   Kilometer   1

0   Mile   1

Fairport Road

490

32 ■ Gazebo

31

Trestle Bridge

Floodgate

Marsh Road

Perinton Park

Church Street Bridge

Widewater Area

Ayrault Road

Palmyra Road

Ayrault Road Bridge

Palmyra Road Bridge

31

Great Embankment Park

Floodgate

East Street

Great Embankment Ends

Spillway

Marsh Road

Bushnell's Basin

Pittsford Victor Road

490

1.5 Reach Great Embankment Park. A mile long and 70 feet high, the Great Embankment was hand-constructed by men with shovels in 1822 to keep the canal from draining into the Irondequoit Creek Valley. It persists in this purpose today, and the Town of Pittsford has added a pleasant, grassy park with picnic tables and benches. This is a nice place to stop and rest.

2.1 A neighborhood connector trail goes off to the left here. Continue straight.

2.3 The Great Embankment ends.

2.4 Notice the water cascading down a stepped spillway to your left.

2.6 To your left, there's road access through a parking lot. If you're hiking in winter, you will certainly notice that from this point on, the Town of Perinton has cleared the snow from the trail.

2.7 The Marsh Road bridge crosses the canal overhead. You can access the bridge using a path to the left of the trail (after you pass under the bridge). Across the canal from here, the mercantile area for Bushnell's Basin, a hamlet of Perinton, offers services including Finger Lakes Coffee Roasters, Abbott's Frozen Custard, more restaurants, and restrooms at the Mobil service station.

3.0 I-490 passes overhead. Continue straight.

3.4 On your right is the second floodgate you'll pass on this walk.

3.9 Pass under the Palmyra Road bridge. If you like, you can access the road using the paths on the left, on either side of the bridge.

4.3 Ayrault Road passes overhead. You can access the road using the paths on either side of the bridge, to your left.

4.6 Wooden stairs to your left lead down into a Perinton neighborhood.

4.9 Reach Fullam's Basin, one of the widest points in the canal. When a canal improvement project shortened and straightened the route in the mid-1800s, crews built a straight embankment across an old loop in the canal at this point, allowing the water to fill in the difference. The result was this "widewater," a favorite stop for tour boats. A stairway to your left leads to the right-of-way for the high-tension wires that pass overhead. People often walk or cross-country ski through this wide swath of clear land. Continue straight on the canal path.

5.4 To the left, an access path leads into a residential neighborhood. Continue straight; you are now passing into Fairport.

5.7 Cross under the Church Street bridge. Perinton Park is straight ahead.

6.0 Arrive in Perinton Park. If you planned a shuttle hike, you'll find your second car in the parking lot here. You may wish to walk (or drive) another 0.5 mile into the village of Fairport, where you will find services including restaurants, the Moonlight Creamery, and Fairport Coffee.

33 Ganondagan State Historic Site: The Earth Is Our Mother Trail

Visit the site of a seventeenth-century Native American village and learn how the Seneca people found many everyday uses for the plants that grow here naturally.

Start: Seneca Art & Culture Center
Distance: 2.0 miles out and back
Hiking time: About 1.5 hours
Elevation gain: 177 feet
High point: 822 feet (at start of trail)
Difficulty: Easy
Best season: Spring and summer, when wild-flowers are in bloom
Traffic: Hikers only

Fees and permits: No fees or permits required to hike the trail; fees to enter longhouse and Seneca Art & Culture Center
Maps: Downloadable GPS track available at ganondagan.org/Visit/Hiking-Trails/Self-Guided-Medicine-Walk
Trail contacts: Ganondagan State Historic Site, 7000 CR 41 (Boughton Hill Road), Victor 14564; (585) 398-6151; ganondagan.org

Finding the trailhead: From the New York State Thruway (I-90), take exit 44 to Canandaigua and follow NY 332 South into Victor. At the third traffic light in Victor (Maple Avenue), turn right onto Boughton Hill Road (CR 41). At the top of the hill, continue straight at the flashing red light. The visitor parking entrance is the second driveway on your right. Park and find the trailhead at the split-rail fence. GPS: N42 57.675' / W77 24.796'

The Hike

The Earth Is Our Mother Trail is part of the self-guided Medicine Walk here at Ganondagan, and one of the most fascinating trails in the greater Rochester area. Its mile-long meander takes you down a gentle slope to Great Brook while providing an intriguing lesson in the native plants the Seneca used for food, medicine, and the creation of household goods. Plaques identify more than twenty plants and trees along the route, providing their names in English and in Seneca, with a quick overview of the uses the native peoples found for each species.

While the plaques make it easy to spot these plants and trees, we do recommend that you bring a field guide with you. Not all of these plants bloom at once, so you may catch a few species in bloom and miss others—unless you walk this trail repeatedly throughout spring and summer, an activity you certainly will find both pleasant and educational. Some plants—especially the trees—will be more recognizable by their fruit, cones, or seeds (think of the maple "propellers" that drop every year in spring and early fall), so a walk at a different time of year may reveal a tree's identity at a glance. Your field guide will help you learn what to watch for as you pass through the forest and fields at Ganondagan.

While the route out descends to the brook and the route back is almost entirely uphill, this walk still belongs in the "easy" category. You will walk a gentle slope at an unhurried pace, with plenty of opportunities to stop and study the plant life, listen for birdsong or the tapping of a woodpecker, and enjoy the rustling of leaves over your head. This trail encourages walkers to slow down and consider what came before us—not the people who perished in a battle, as so many of New York's trails remind

Historical Background

Part of the Haudenosaunee (what we know as the Iroquois), the Seneca nation occupied the westernmost territory inhabited by this Native American confederacy. Ganondagan stood as the largest Seneca town, a place where villagers grew the "three sisters" crops—corn, beans, and squash—and lived a quiet life between skirmishes with rival tribes in the area.

This was the status quo until Ganondagan became the center of peacemaking activities between the original five nations of the Iroquois Confederacy: the Mohawk, Onondaga, Oneida, Cayuga, and Seneca.

A man known as the Great Peacemaker—a prophet named Dekanawida, who may have come from a Huron tribe farther west (though some say he was an Onondaga raised by Mohawk parents)—brought the five nations together by calling for an end to rivalries among the tribes, employing his friend and orator Hiawatha to make the case. The Peacemaker also worked closely with a woman of Ganondagan named Jikonsase, who opened her home to the first meeting of the leaders of each nation. The Mohawk, Oneida, and Cayuga saw the value of the federation first, but the Seneca responded with violence and conflict . . . until a day when the sky darkened and the sun went black and night seemed to fall in the middle of the day. This phenomenon was probably a solar eclipse, but it made a dramatic impact on the Seneca, who took it as a sign that they should join the Haudenosaunee.

Historians have determined that these events probably took place in 1451. More than 200 years later, the peaceful Seneca nation encountered its first Europeans, and the fate of this farming community took a turn for the worse.

First came the missionaries in 1656, including Father Pierre-Joseph-Marie Chaumont, who preached the Jesuit gospel to the Seneca and sent other representatives

(Continued)

to convert the "savages" to Christianity. The Seneca nation rejected the tenets forced upon them and eventually drove the missionaries out of Ganondagan in 1684.

Meanwhile, British officials arrived in the area and met with the Iroquois nations, securing a friendship with them on behalf of England. This angered the French in the area, who already saw the Seneca as competitors in the fur trade and hardly needed a reason to engage them in conflict. On June 13, 1687, Marquis de Denonville led a fighting force of more than 2,000 men—French and Canadian soldiers and some 400 Indians from other tribes—into New York to attack the Seneca. The resulting battles, known as the Beaver Wars, would decide who dominated the fur trade from that day forward.

The Seneca knew the French were on their way and assembled a force of 800 men and women, meeting the French militia north of Ganondagan. A skirmish ensued, but the Seneca soon determined that they were suffering significant casualties. The Seneca retreated—but before the battle, they had moved all the residents of Ganondagan to safety in Cayuga. As the French forces closed in on the Seneca village, they found it in flames. The Seneca had set fire to it rather than allow the French to take it from them. They could not move thousands of bushels of corn stored in their warehouses, however, so the French destroyed those, driving the Seneca out of the area and securing the fur trade for themselves.

Ganondagan is now a National Historic Landmark and a State Historic Site, a place where you can see a reconstructed Seneca longhouse and learn more about a piece of history that has maintained a fairly low profile. With the opening of the new Seneca Art & Culture Center here in the fall of 2015, the story of the Seneca nation emerges as a key element in New York State's colorful past.

us, but the people who lived, farmed, hunted and gathered, and made a home on this land centuries before Europeans landed on the East Coast and began to make their way west.

Miles and Directions

0.0 Start at the parking area and proceed to the trailhead at the split-rail fence. Cross a mowed meadow and pass the new Seneca Art & Culture Center on your left. Begin the marked Trail of Peace by going toward the bark longhouse.

Tour an Iroquois longhouse before hiking the Earth Is Our Mother Trail at Ganondagan State Historic Site.

Ganondagan State Historic Site: The Earth Is Our Mother Trail

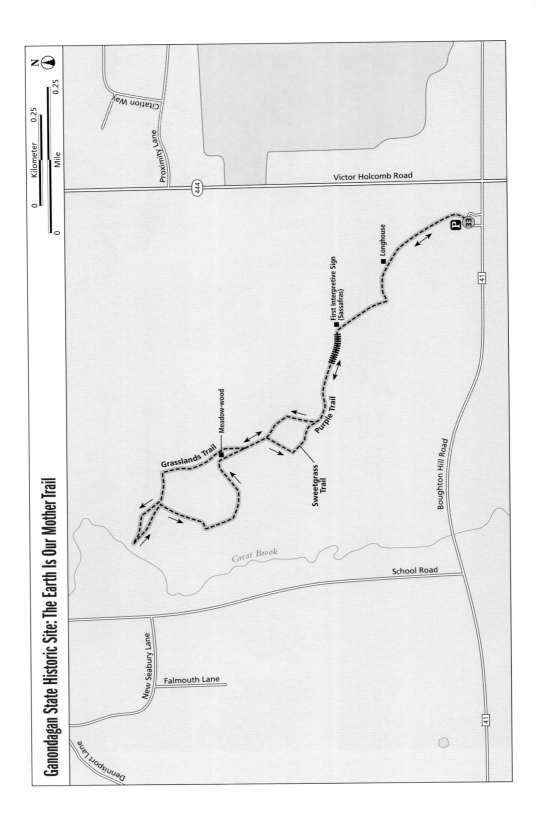

0.2 Reach the bark longhouse. Bear left into the woods. You will see two trails here: One is the paved trail to the new center; the other is a dirt trail into the woods. Take the dirt trail. You can see a purple trail marker ahead of you.

0.3 At the end of a gradual descent, the first interpretive sign points out the sassafras shrub. Watch for these signs to help you differentiate the trees and plants along the route. A boardwalk soon begins. At the end of the boardwalk, bear right.

0.4 Come to another boardwalk.

0.5 Bear left at the trail junction, following the purple markers. (You'll follow the other trail on the way back.) In a moment you'll meet the end of the red-blazed trail; bear right.

0.6 At the end of the Sweetgrass Fork, bear left.

0.7 The Meadow-wood Fork goes right. Continue straight.

0.9 The Meadow-wood Fork goes right. Stay left. Shortly, the Cottonwood Trail goes right. Stay left.

1.0 The trail ends at Great Brook. Return the way you came, taking the side trails as you wish.

1.1 The Meadow-wood Fork goes right. Turn right here.

1.3 Rejoin the main trail by turning right. Shortly, take the Sweetgrass Trail you skipped before.

1.4 Complete the Sweetgrass Trail and continue uphill, following the purple markers back to the longhouse.

1.8 Arrive back at the longhouse. Take the Trail of Peace back to the parking area.

2.0 Arrive back at the parking area.

34 Mount Hope Cemetery

Follow a path through the final resting place of more than 350,000 people, and discover the captains of industry and crusaders for human rights who once lived and worked in Rochester.

Start: Entrance to Mount Hope Cemetery, between Reservoir and Robinson Avenues on Mount Hope Avenue in Rochester
Distance: 1.0-mile loop
Hiking time: About 35 minutes
Elevation gain: 150 feet
High point: 638 feet
Difficulty: Easy
Best season: Spring and fall
Traffic: Hikers, cyclists, slow-moving cars

Fees and permits: No fees or permits required
Maps: Available at the 1874 gatehouse at the entrance to the cemetery
Trail contacts: Mount Hope Cemetery, 1133 Mount Hope Ave., Rochester 14620; (585) 428-7999; cityofrochester.gov/mounthope
Special considerations: This is an active cemetery, so it's very likely you will come across a funeral during your visit. Please be respectful of the mourners and pass by them quietly.

Finding the trailhead: The cemetery entrance is at 791 Mount Hope Ave. in Rochester. From I-390, take exit 17 for Scottsville Road (NY 383). Follow the signs for Rochester and merge onto NY 383 going north. Bear right onto Elmwood Avenue and continue 0.8 mile to Mount Hope Avenue. Turn left onto Mount Hope and continue to the second entrance for Mount Hope Cemetery. GPS: N43 08.056' / W77 36.879'

The Hike

Quiet, peaceful, and remarkably picturesque, Mount Hope Cemetery offers one of the most fascinating and informative hiking experiences in Rochester—and for a city with as many hiking trails as this one, that's quite a statement. Shaded with hundred-year-old trees, crisscrossed with cobblestone and brick driving lanes, and dotted with more extravagant statuary than a Civil War battlefield, this remarkable cemetery provides a one-of-a-kind hiking adventure.

This fairly short walk packs considerable historical punch, taking you into the oldest part of the cemetery to discover the final resting places of women's rights activist Susan B. Anthony, abolitionist and orator Frederick Douglass, inventors Hiram Sibley and Seth Green, and monuments to John Jacob Bausch and Henry Lomb. You'll find a mausoleum dedicated to philanthropist Margaret Woodbury Strong, a stunning monument to world-renowned horticulturalist George Ellwanger, and the gatehouse, gazebo, fountain, and original crematory, all dating back to the 1870s.

Beyond these familiar names, the graves of many other interesting people can be found in Mount Hope Cemetery. An exploration of the expansive acreage south of this hike takes you to Jacob Myers, inventor of the voting machine; publisher Frank Gannett; pharmaceutical scientist and philanthropist Edwin G. Strasenburgh;

Rochester's Fathers of Invention

Not only has Rochester produced people who changed the course of history, but the city has also turned out many captains of industry, a number of whom are buried in Mount Hope Cemetery.

Here you will find the grave of Seth Green—not the actor, but the developer of a technique for artificial propagation of fish. Green founded the first fish hatchery in nearby Caledonia, and his methods soon became useful in rehabilitating depleted fish populations in compromised lakes and rivers.

In 1853 John Jacob Bausch, an immigrant from Germany, borrowed $60 from his friend Henry Lomb to help fund his optical goods business. Bausch & Lomb made rubber eyeglass frames—a brand-new concept at the time—and by the early 1900s the company held patents for binoculars, microscopes, and other precision optics. The company's long history and wide range of products are now common knowledge, and its founders rest here beneath monuments that bear their names.

Rochester residents tend to associate the name Sibley with the locally owned (now defunct) department store that anchored downtown Rochester for many decades. Hiram Sibley, the man who is buried here, actually was a pioneer in the advancement of the telegraph, creating the New York and Mississippi Valley Printing Telegraph Company here in Rochester. Sibley later became the first president of Western Union, and he worked with partners to found the Pacific Telegraph Company, providing a communication link between the East and West Coasts of the United States for the first time.

the children of Buffalo Bill Cody; and thousands of soldiers who died in the Civil War, the Spanish-American War, and World War I.

If you'd like to know a great deal more about the cemetery and the people buried here than we can fit into this chapter, we highly recommend taking one of the tours hosted by Friends of Mount Hope Cemetery, a nonprofit organization dedicated to preserving this cultural resource. Tours are given on Sunday spring through fall, and the tour guides can answer all kinds of questions about the famous (and not-so-famous) people buried or entombed at Mount Hope. For more information about tours, visit fomh.org.

Historical Background

Dedicated in 1838, Mount Hope Cemetery became the nation's first municipal Victorian cemetery—a designation that may not mean much until you set eyes on this striking, monument-studded landscape. When the City of Rochester bought the first 54 acres here and dedicated it as a cemetery, a movement had just gained momentum in London, England, to create cemeteries beyond those in churchyards in the city center. London's church burial sites had become so overcrowded that they actually threatened public health, but the city's government had not moved to address the matter. Instead, private organizations took on the challenge of creating new suburban cemeteries in and around London, founding some of the most famous cemeteries of the Victorian era.

Rochester observed this activity and determined that there were benefits to having a large city-based cemetery with municipal oversight. Its leaders took a page from London's book and made a landscaped burial space with a decorative entrance, an elaborate chapel and crematorium in the style of the period, and a gatehouse that still invites admiration by visitors.

Glaciers carved out 196 acres of hills and valleys here, and the people of Rochester filled them with more than 350,000 graves—a number that continues to grow daily in this very active cemetery. The more that people used the cemetery space, the more they discovered that they enjoyed the rolling hills, ancient trees, well-tended gardens, and views of the Genesee River. Picnics at Mount Hope Cemetery became a favorite weekend pastime, and residents drove through at a leisurely pace, first in horse-drawn carriages and eventually in automobiles. Memorial Day became a local event, with people in their Sunday finery bringing wreaths and other tributes to their deceased loved ones and then staying for band concerts and more picnicking.

Even today, a warm-weather weekend brings families with strollers, couples, and groups of visitors to Mount Hope Cemetery to find their way to the most famous graves in this parklike setting. Two of the most celebrated people buried here were actually good friends in their lifetimes: Susan B. Anthony, considered the founder of the women's suffrage movement in the United States and a lifelong Rochester resident, and Frederick Douglass, an escaped slave who became one of the most sought-after orators and authors of his time, traveling the country to urge abolition of slavery in the Southern states. Douglass settled in Rochester in 1847 and lived here with his family for twenty-five years, until his home on South Avenue burned to the ground in 1872. He chose Rochester because of Anthony, whom he had met on a speaking tour, and here he produced his newspaper, the *North Star* (later the *Frederick Douglass Paper*). In 1848 Douglass was the only man to attend the first Women's Rights Convention in Seneca Falls.

Anthony also published her own newspaper, the *Revolution*, here in her home on Madison Street, and she fought tirelessly for women's right to vote, even going so far as to attempt to vote in 1872 and spending time in jail for doing so. Anthony raised the funds required by the University of Rochester to open its doors to female students for the first time, and she worked to abolish slavery and to give women legal rights when they were abused by drunken husbands. Although she died in 1906, fourteen years before passage of the Nineteenth Amendment, she left the suffrage movement one of its most inspiring phrases: "Failure is impossible." History credits her work alongside fellow activist Elizabeth Cady Stanton with the eventual passage of this amendment.

Women's rights movement leader Susan B. Anthony is buried in Rochester's Mount Hope Cemetery.

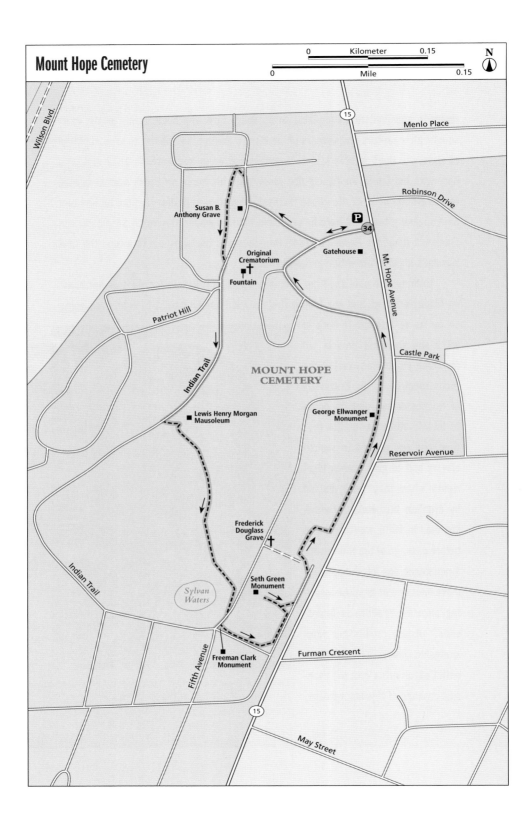

Mount Hope Cemetery

0   Kilometer   0.15

0   Mile   0.15

N

Wilson Blvd.

Menlo Place

Robinson Drive

15

P

34

Susan B. Anthony Grave

Original Crematorium

Gatehouse

Fountain

Mt. Hope Avenue

Patriot Hill

Castle Park

Indian Trail

MOUNT HOPE CEMETERY

Lewis Henry Morgan Mausoleum

George Ellwanger Monument

Reservoir Avenue

Frederick Douglass Grave

Indian Trail

Sylvan Waters

Seth Green Monument

Furman Crescent

Fifth Avenue

Freeman Clark Monument

15

May Street

Miles and Directions

0.0 Start at the main gate at 791 Mount Hope Ave. The 1874 gatehouse is to your left; the fountain is straight ahead. To your right you can see the gazebo and the grave of Hiram Sibley. Take the cobblestone road to your right. This becomes Indian Trail. When Indian Trail meets Linden Road, turn right on Linden. Continue to the paved path, just past the small directional signs for Susan B. Anthony's grave. Follow the signs.

0.1 Come to the Anthony family plot. You can also see one building in this area—the Woodbury family mausoleum, where Margaret Woodbury Strong was laid to rest. Continue to the end of the gravel path, rejoining the Indian Trail.

0.2 Turn right on the Indian Trail and go up the hill.

0.4 Turn left onto Hope Avenue.

0.5 At the end of Hope, turn right and then continue straight as the road splits around the Freeman Clarke monument. Bear left and take the next left. Turn left again at the road along the fence.

0.6 When you see a paved path, turn left and proceed straight to the Seth Green monument (the tall statue with the robed orator at the top). When you're ready, return to the road, turn left, and continue to the concrete steps.

0.7 You can see a marker for Frederick Douglass's grave. Take the steps and gravel path, and follow the markers to the gravesite. When you're ready, return to the road and continue to your left.

0.8 Reach the monument to George Ellwanger. Continue straight through the next intersection (East and Prospect). East turns left and becomes Lawn Avenue. Continue on Lawn to return to your vehicle.

1.0 Arrive back at the gate and your vehicle.

35 Highland Park

The nation's largest and most diverse collection of lilacs highlights this Frederick Law Olmsted–designed park, the jewel of Monroe County's park system.

Start: Purple crosswalk on Highland Avenue, between South Goodman Street and South Avenue in the city of Rochester
Distance: 1.1-mile loop
Hiking time: About 40 minutes
Elevation gain: 103 feet
High point: 650 feet
Difficulty: Easy
Best season: May, when the lilacs are blooming

Traffic: Hikers, families with children
Fees and permits: No fees or permits required
Maps: Park map available at monroecounty .gov/File/HighlandPark(1).pdf
Trail contacts: Monroe County Parks Department, 100 Reservoir Ave., Rochester 14620; (585) 271-5420; monroecounty.gov/parks-highland.php

Finding the trailhead: From I-490 in Rochester, take the Culver Road exit. Turn south on Culver Road and continue to Monroe Avenue. Turn left onto Monroe and continue to the next traffic light at Highland Avenue. Turn right at the light and continue about 1 mile to the intersection with Goodman Avenue. Highland Park begins here. Continue straight across Goodman, pass the pansy bed on your right, and find parking (free for 2 hours) on Highland Avenue near the purple-painted crosswalk. GPS: N43 07.784' / W77 36.497'

The Hike

I've got to come clean from the start: Highland Park during lilac season is my favorite place on Earth. I've had the pleasure of serving as spokesperson for the Rochester Lilac Festival, a ten-day event that draws more than 500,000 people to the park in May, so I know what this park means to the people of the City of Rochester and Monroe County. I hope you will forgive the bias I bring to this chapter, and that you will find Highland Park to be every bit as extraordinary as I describe it here.

Beginning at the purple crosswalk—a crossing that gets a fresh coat of lilac–colored paint every other year—this walk wanders through the collection of more than 1,200 lilac plants, representing more than 500 varieties, many of which were developed here in Rochester by the city's and county's horticulturalists. Most of the lilacs usually bloom during the second and third weeks of May, but some late bloomers won't burst their buds until mid-June, so you have an excellent chance of enjoying the sight and equally delicious scent of these flowers throughout the last days of spring.

This path not only leads along the top edge of the lilac collection but also winds through many other varieties of flowering trees and shrubs, as well as wildflowers

Enjoy Olmsted's inspired design on a stroll through Highland Park. ▶

Frederick Law Olmsted in New York

Considered the father of landscape architecture, Frederick Law Olmsted began his career with a high-profile project: New York City's Central Park, one of the crowning achievements of park design in the middle of a massive urban center. Olmsted worked with his more-experienced partner, English architect Calvert Vaux, to design a green space that would be accessible to people from every social class and walk of life, creating the first true "public park." Olmsted and Vaux went on to design Prospect Park in New York City and Chicago's Riverside parks before they were asked to work with the city of Buffalo, New York, on its burgeoning park system.

In Buffalo Olmsted created the first-ever system of parks linked by interconnecting parkways, including Cazenovia, Delaware, Front, Humboldt, Riverside, South, and Day's Parks, as well as Bennett Park, Masten Place, and The Terrace, which were lost to development over time. The system of parkways and circles made it easy for residents to ride carriages or automobiles through the entire city and enjoy the landscaped spaces preserved for that purpose.

Olmsted went on to design the Niagara Reservation at Niagara Falls and eventually the "emerald necklace" of four city parks in Rochester: Seneca Park along the Genesee River Gorge; Maplewood Park with its extraordinary rose garden; Genesee Valley Park and its rolling pastoral fields; and the hills, valleys, and spectacular gardens of Highland Park.

and cultivated varieties at ground level. The route detailed here takes you through the gardens of azalea (a May bloomer) and rhododendron (June's crowning glory), and along beds of annuals and perennials that create a brilliant landscape throughout the warmer months. Something is blooming any time of year in this park—even in late fall and winter, when witch hazel sports its yellow flowers and adds spice to the aroma of raked leaves.

Continuing through the park, sets of stairs take you to overlooks that provide a wide view of Frederick Law Olmsted's vision for this park, and to the reservoir that has supplied water from Hemlock and Canadice Lakes to city residents since 1875. You'll also walk through the Pinetum (that's pine-AY-tum), an area planted with 300 different species of coniferous (cone-bearing) trees from all over the world, and on into a mowed, shady valley lined with leafy trees including maple, horse chestnut, dogwood, cherry, several varieties of oak, ash, and others.

The route takes you to the deck of Lamberton Conservatory, built in 1911 and restored and expanded in 2007. The new 1,800-square-foot facility provides displays of exotic plants that thrive in tropical and desert environments as well as epiphytes, orchids, ferns, a koi pond, a room of house plants, and seasonal displays. The conservatory is open every day except Christmas, and a stop here really tops off the entire experience of touring Highland Park.

Historical Background

We have the foresight and consummate skills of George Ellwanger and Patrick Barry, two prominent Rochester citizens in 1887 and national thought leaders in horticultural science, to thank for the creation of Highland Park. Not only did these two gentlemen donate 19.63 acres of their own land to create the park, but they insisted that, as part of the agreement to donate the land, the city hire a professional landscape engineer to develop this park.

The following year, the New York State Legislature took a bold step, creating the City of Rochester Parks Commission to oversee all the open spaces planned for this upstate commercial center. The move came as a growing number of city and state officials began to see the value in creating parks within cities—places where people could congregate for city-sponsored events, take a leisurely stroll on a Sunday afternoon, and enjoy a natural landscape as a haven from the crush of industrial activity around them.

In 1893 the World's Columbian Exposition took place in Chicago, drawing 27 million visitors and featuring a landscape designed by an enlightened architect, Frederick Law Olmsted. Using the natural landscape of Chicago's Jackson Park, Olmsted took advantage of nearby Lake Michigan to create a series of lagoons and waterways that served as reflecting pools and means of transportation. Olmsted's vision transformed the way people saw parks within cities, creating a demand for oases of shade trees, quiet brooks, green lawns, and showy displays of flowering plants.

This is the vision Olmsted brought first to Buffalo's Delaware Park and then to Rochester for a chain of three parks—Highland, Genesee Valley, and Seneca. Although he was initially disappointed that Highland Park would not have a

(Continued)

free-flowing natural water feature, he found the existing topography of the glacial moraine—the dips and rises of the park's valleys and hillsides—most interesting and useful. He turned the high ground east of the reservoir into a place to view the entire landscape, creating a three-story structure known for many decades as the Children's Pavilion. (The pavilion fell into disrepair and was demolished in the 1960s.) We can still experience the vista Olmsted intended for us, though the trees in front of the elevated deck have grown considerably since the architect's days, obscuring some of the view.

On the park's southern slope, Olmsted carefully placed flowering shrubs and trees, choosing the lilacs that would become the park's most famous collection. Lilacs are cold-hardy plants that fare very well through the dormancy of an upstate New York winter, and the showy panicles of tiny purple, pink, ivory, or white flowers give off a heady scent that has come to mean spring to sun-starved Rochesterians.

Finally, don't miss the pansy bed near the corner of Highland Avenue and South Goodman Street. Hand-planted every spring with more than 10,000 individual pansy plants, the bed sports a different symmetrical design each year, making it an annual stopping place for local residents and visitors. Once the pansies have played out, the park's horticulturalists replace them with a wide range of annuals from petunias to cannas, giving the garden a second life that lasts until the snow flies.

Miles and Directions

0.0 Start at the purple crosswalk and cross to the north side of the street. Follow the paved path through the lilac collection. Turn right at the T intersection.

0.2 At the intersection with a trail to the left, continue straight.

0.3 At the next intersection, turn left. (**Option:** Going straight takes you to the corner of Highland and Goodman; this is a good way to reach the pansy bed.)

0.5 Come to the rhododendron collection. At the next intersection, turn right; then go straight up the steps. (The path to the right leads to Goodman Street.) At the top of the steps, bear left toward the overlook.

0.6 Reach the overlook, which has grown up considerably since Olmsted's day. Continue to the right to see the reservoir. There are benches and picnic tables here if you want to linger to enjoy the view. To your right, there's another platform with a view into the Pinetum. Stairs from here lead down to another landing.

Highland Park

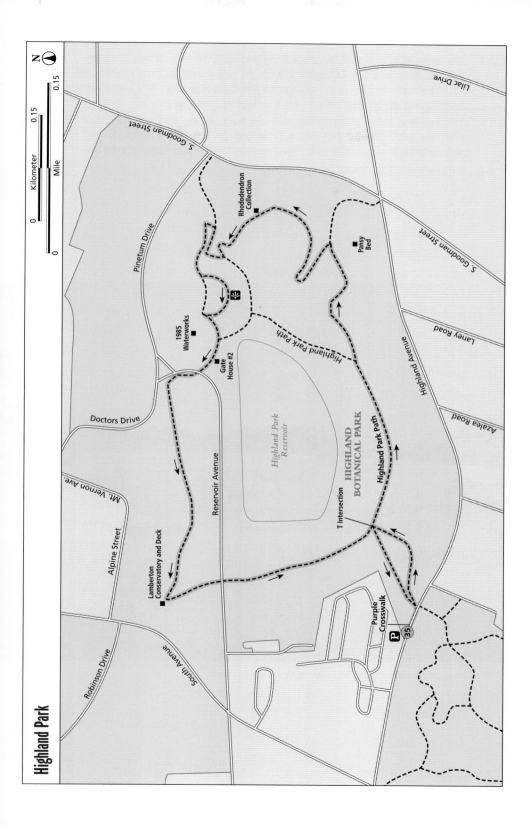

0.7 Gate House #2 is to the left. The 1985 Waterworks building is on your right. Continue straight to Reservoir Road. Turn right and follow the road around the curve until you see the dirt path into the gully. (If you get to Alpine Road, you've gone too far.) Turn left on this path and descend between the trees into a valley with mowed grass.

1.0 Stairs here lead to Lamberton Conservatory. Take the stairs, and stop on the landing for a nice view of the gully and the Pinetum. Cross Reservoir Road at the crosswalk, and continue straight on the paved path. (Don't miss the hollowed-out tree to your right.)

1.1 Arrive back at the purple crosswalk.

The reservoir at Highland Park provides water to city residents.

Western New York

View New York's Southern Tier from the platform at Newtown Battlefield.

36 Royalton Ravine County Park

Hike to the bottom of a hidden ravine, cross a swaying cable extension bridge over a rushing stream, and ascend to the top of a four-season waterfall on this lushly wooded, secluded trail.

Start: End of the gravel road in Victor A. Fitchlee Park, Gasport
Distance: 2.5-mile loop or 3.0 miles out and back
Hiking time: About 1.25 hours
Elevation gain: 178 feet
High point: 631 feet
Difficulty: Moderate

Best season: Apr through Nov
Traffic: Hikers only
Fees and permits: No fees or permits required
Maps: National Geographic Topo! New York State edition
Trail contact: Niagara County Parks, 59 Park Ave., Lockport 14094; (716) 439-7950; niagaracounty.com/Parks

Finding the trailhead: From Buffalo take the New York State Thruway (I-90) East to exit 49 (Depew). At the end of the exit ramp, turn north (left) onto Transit Road (NY 78). In 15.3 miles, turn right (east) onto NY 31 and continue about 17 miles to Lockport. Bear right to stay on NY 31 and drive 6.5 miles to Gasport Road. Turn right onto Gasport and watch for the sign for Victor A. Fitchlee Park (Royalton Ravine). Park in the parking lot near the trailhead. GPS: N43 11.185' / W78 34.629'

The Hike

A delightful, secluded place within Niagara County, Royalton Ravine—created by the flow of the Eastern Branch of Eighteenmile Creek over thousands of years—offers a chance to view a 100-foot-deep cross section of the county's fascinating geology. Even more fun than that, however, is the bridge over the creek at the bottom of the ravine, a swaying 195-foot expanse of wooden planks suspended from cables. Safe and sturdy, the bridge nonetheless provides a sense that you're adventuring in an untamed wilderness, with the ravine's walls rising behind and in front of you and the creek's waters burbling below as you teeter your way across.

Vague trail markings and confusing combinations of blazes and metal markers will add mystique to your hike, but it's worth sorting through them to reach this park's hidden enchantments. A short side trail takes you to the edge of the creek's wetland watershed; a steady descent leads to the bottom and the bridge; and the resulting ascent guides you to the sound of rushing water, ravine walls wet with spring runoff, and a 70-foot cascade that delivers cleansing spray to the rocks that surround it.

You can reach the cascade—appropriately named Royalton Falls—more quickly by parking on Kayner Road and taking a short trail that leads in from the road, but

Historical Background

Don't miss the ruins of a stone building that stand just before the spur trail to the cascade. Belva Ann Bennett Lockwood, the first woman to practice law before the US Supreme Court, was born in this modest homestead on the edge of the ravine on October 24, 1830. Married at 18 and widowed five years later, Lockwood realized that she needed an education to support herself and her 3-year-old daughter, so she attended Genesee Wesleyan Seminary amid the objections of her friends and relatives, most of whom believed that it was unseemly for a woman to pursue higher education—and virtually unheard of for a widow to do so. Determined to be self-sufficient, however, she graduated and became the headmistress of Lockport Union School, a position in which she was paid half the salary her male counterparts received.

When she met women's rights activist Susan B. Anthony in 1864, Lockwood's views on the possibilities for women changed dramatically. She made additions to the curricula of the schools in which she taught, bringing in courses that would prepare female students for careers beyond domestic life or teaching. Lockwood (whose last name was McNall at the time) moved to Washington, DC, where she met her second husband, the Reverend Ezekiel Lockwood, and became an active women's suffragist. She earned a law degree from what is now George Washington University Law School, and when the university refused her a diploma because it didn't give diplomas to women, she wrote to President Ulysses S. Grant, an ex-president of the university, and demanded justice. A week later, her diploma arrived.

Gaining some visibility as an attorney and a crusader for women's rights, Lockwood became the first woman to run for president of the United States in 1884 and again in 1888, the nominee of the short-lived Equal Rights Party. As women did not gain the right to vote in national elections until 1921, Lockwood did not have a serious chance of winning the presidency, but she did garner 4,100 votes from male voters—a significant feat at the time. (Voters in Oregon and Pennsylvania reported seeing votes for Lockwood dumped into wastebaskets uncounted or torn up in front of their faces, so her voters may well have been much more numerous.) Today Lockwood is buried in the Congressional Cemetery in Washington, a final testament to her importance as a political figure. In 1983 she was honored with induction into the National Women's Hall of Fame in Seneca Falls, New York.

The suspension bridge at the bottom of Royalton Ravine makes this a favorite hike with children.

you'll miss the fun of the ravine descent through mature forest and the swaying foot-bridge, as well as the great quad workout you'll get on the ascent.

Miles and Directions

0.0 Start at the end of the gravel road in the park, where you'll find a trail map displayed. Follow along the edge of the ravine/creek until you reach the woods.

0.2 Enter the woods. Follow the yellow-painted metal squares on the trees; these are the trail markers.

0.4 The yellow-marked trail ends here, at a spot called the "wildlife blind." There's no actual blind structure, but you'll be hidden by vegetation if you want to observe wildlife in this marshy area. When you're ready, retrace your steps to the intersection of the yellow- and orange-marked trails.

0.5 Turn right and continue uphill on the yellow/orange trail (it's tough to distinguish one color marker from the other, so follow both). You may see yellow or orange ribbons on trees as part of the trail markings.

0.7 The red- and yellow-marked trails meet here; continue straight. From here, painted blazes replace the metal markers for the most part. Watch for a set of steps with a yellow propylene rope as a handrail. Go down the steps.

0.8 The cable suspension bridge begins here. Cross the bridge, which is just under 200 feet long. When you're across, begin a steady but gentle ascent to the top of the ravine.

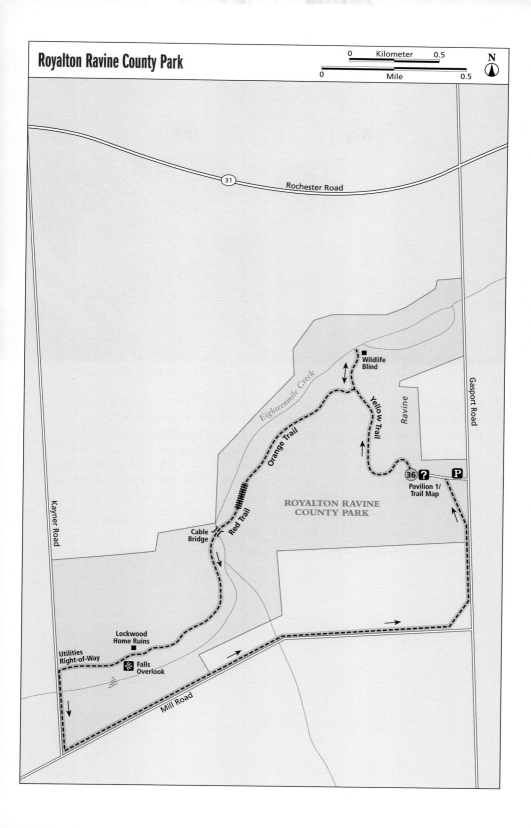

Royalton Ravine County Park

0   Kilometer   0.5

0   Mile   0.5

N

Rochester Road

31

Gasport Road

Eighteenmile Creek

Wildlife Blind

Yellow Trail

Ravine

Orange Trail

36 ? P

Pavilion 1/
Trail Map

Cable
Bridge

Red Trail

ROYALTON RAVINE
COUNTY PARK

Kayner Road

Lockwood
Home Ruins

Utilities
Right-of-Way

Falls
Overlook

Mill Road

Trout lilies carpet the floor of Royalton Ravine in spring.

1.1   Watch for the ruins of Belva Lockwood's home here. Royalton Falls is coming up on the left. Take the short trail to the left for a great view of the falls. (Watch your step!)

1.3   Cross the right-of-way for high-tension wires and the county gas line and reach Kayner Road. (**Option:** You can turn around here and retrace your steps through the ravine and back to the parking lot or walk along the roads back to the park. The distance is about the same either way.) If you're taking the road to complete the loop, turn left here on Kayner and walk to the next intersection.

1.5   Turn left onto Mill Road. Continue to Gasport Road, where you'll turn left.

2.3   Turn left onto Gasport Road and return to the park.

2.5   Arrive back at the park; continue to the parking lot.

37 Devil's Hole State Park

A winding descent on a 200-foot rock staircase, a trek along the Niagara River's edge, and a chance to peer inside a huge side gorge are just some of the adventures on this eventful hike.

Start: Devil's Hole Trailhead on the Robert Moses Parkway, just north of the Niagara Falls Discovery Center
Distance: 2.5-mile loop
Hiking time: About 2 hours
Elevation gain: 533 feet
High point: 578 feet (at the trailhead)
Difficulty: Moderate
Best season: May through Oct
Traffic: Hikers only
Fees and permits: No fees or permits required

Maps: Available from the Niagara Falls Gorge Discovery Center and at the trailhead
Trail contact: Regional Park Programs Office, DeVeaux Woods State Park, 3160 DeVeaux Woods Dr., Niagara Falls 14305; (716) 282-5154; niagarafallsstatepark.com
Special considerations: Take special care when hiking in winter. Crampons or other ice-gripping footwear is required to navigate ice-covered paths.

Finding the trailhead: From Niagara Falls, take the Robert Moses Parkway north past the Niagara Gorge Discovery Center to the park. Park in the area across the road from the park, and take the pedestrian walkway over the road to the gorge rim. The trailhead is to the right, near the Niagara Power Project scenic overlook. If you arrive on the parkway from the north, the park entrance is on your right. GPS: N43 07.952' / W79 02.818'

The Hike

Nearly obscured from view until you're standing at its rim, the Devil's Hole area can be startling at first glimpse: a deep gouge in the Niagara Gorge—actually a side gorge, eroded by an outlet of an ancient glacial lake (long since run dry) now filled with thriving vegetation.

You're about to follow a series of stone and concrete staircases around the perimeter of the side gorge, finally coming to ground just a few feet above water level—an extraordinary place from which to view the river's pounding rapids, standing waves, and daunting rock formations.

The steep stairs—some 300 steps in all—are only the beginning of the adventure here. This is an active gorge, where rockfalls are commonplace, so it's likely that the trail will be overrun in some spots by fallen dolostone and other sedimentary rock. Wear sturdy footwear with closed toes, and be prepared to step over piles of shale and sandstone as you make your way along this trail.

If you're up to the challenge, the payoff here is rich. Viewing the river's swirling waters, still agitated from their tumble over Niagara Falls, can be one of upstate New York's sublime wilderness experiences. Rapids in this part of the river are rated Class

III, but you'll see Class V whitewater if you continue past the Whirlpool staircase on the Whirlpool Rapids Trail.

A second set of steps awaits you at the end of the gorge portion of this hike, but these are not as steep, and there are gently inclined switchback trails between

Historical Background

First, the geological history: Devil's Hole is the creation of an ancient glacial lake, which supplied the waterfall that cascaded down the rock face here and wore away the top layers to reveal the sedimentary dolostone beneath it.

When the Seneca tribe of the six nations of the Iroquois Confederacy discovered this gorge before European explorers and settlers arrived in the area, they believed that the Great Spirit had given the land to them with a promise of peace and prosperity. When the Seneca found themselves in conflict with other tribes and their disagreements escalated into battles, their altercations angered the Great Spirit so much that he punished then by moving the Great Falls of Onguiaahra (what we know as Niagara) and by sending storms that rolled boulders away from the rock walls and pushed the river gorge far back from its original location.

This movement released something more than water, according to the legend: The devil who lived in this side gorge became active when the walls moved. Devil's Hole comes with a curse, one that affects anyone who tries to venture deep into the cave behind the rock stairs. Not only did this evil spirit take the lives of several Indians who tried to enter the cave, but it placed a curse on French explorer René-Robert Cavelier, Sieur de La Salle, who ignored all warning from his Seneca guide and entered the cave alone to speak with the spirit. When the wraith told him to return to Canada and prosperity instead of continuing his explorations of the New World, La Salle famously scoffed at the prophecy of disaster and death the spirit described. He went west, and just about every attempt at colonization, exploration, and collection of riches he attempted went sour. La Salle finally died at the hands of his own men on the coast of what would become Texas.

(Continued)

From the Devil's Hole trail, you can see both the US (left) and Canada (right) on the Niagara River.

In 1763, nearly one hundred years after La Salle ventured into Devil's Hole, the French still battled the British for control of the Great Lakes. The Seneca worked closely with the French throughout this seven-year conflict—what Americans know as the French and Indian War—and the French paid them for their loyalty by employing them as supply runners. When the British won the war and built a portage road for wagons and horses, as many as 300 Seneca runners suddenly found themselves out of their jobs. They began to grumble, and that grumbling became a plan for an attack. On September 14, 1763, the Seneca ambushed a wagon train on a strip of land just above Devil's Hole. Panicked horses and cattle upset wagons into the ravine, and twenty-one men from the wagon train died in the battle. British Regulars who heard the commotion soon arrived to assist, but they also fell at the hands of the Seneca, with more than eighty casualties added to the list of the dead and wounded. In contrast, only one Seneca suffered a wound at the Battle of Devil's Hole; otherwise, all 309 men who attacked the British survived the battle.

staircases. You're welcome to retrace your steps down the Devil's Hole Trail to return to your car, but I recommend climbing out of the gorge here at the end and walking back to the trailhead along the Rim Trail at the top. (You will probably choose your return path according to the condition of the trail and whether rockfalls have made parts of it difficult to traverse.)

Miles and Directions

0.0   Start at the parking area and take the pedestrian walkway over the road to the gorge rim. The trailhead is to the right, near the scenic overlook.

0.3   Reach the stairs to the power plant overlook. The largest electricity producer in New York State, the recently modernized Robert Moses Niagara Power Plant diverts water from the river and into the plant, generating 2.4 million kilowatts of carbon-free electricity through the power of water. The stairs down into the gorge begin at the end of this platform.

0.5   You've come down 0.2 mile of stairs to the trail, just above water level. Turn left and begin to follow the trail along the river gorge. There are some narrow points in the trail with steep drop-offs, and some areas are obscured by fallen rock. Huge boulders may seem to block the trail, but the path usually winds between them.

1.3   Reach Giant Rock, an impressive chunk of dolostone fallen from the Lockport Formation above you. (From the Canadian side of the river, you can see the hole in the wall that this rock once occupied.)

1.5   Come to the Whirlpool staircase at the end of the Devil's Hole Trail. The Whirlpool Rapids Trail continues straight ahead—a challenging hike, with some boulder hopping. (**Option:**

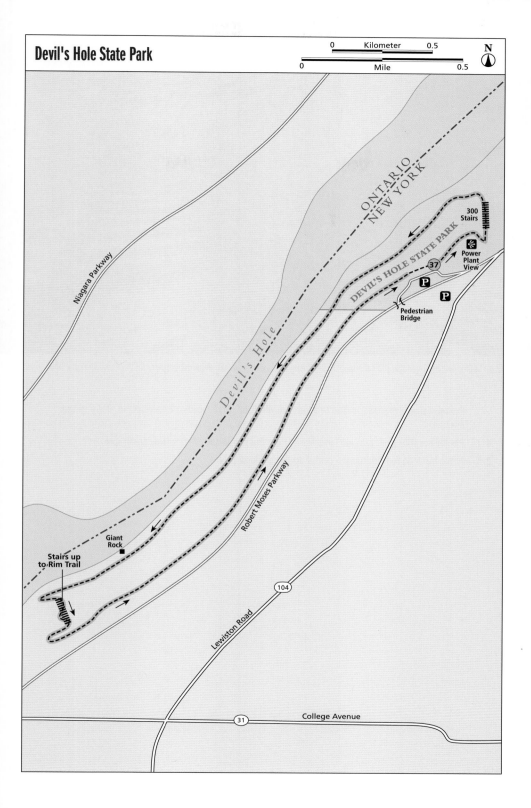

Devil's Hole State Park

Kilometer

0   0.5

Mile

0   0.5

N

ONTARIO
NEW YORK

DEVIL'S HOLE STATE PARK

Devil's Hole

Niagara Parkway

Robert Moses Parkway

Lewiston Road

300
Stairs

Power
Plant
View

37

P

P

Pedestrian
Bridge

Giant
Rock

Stairs up
to Rim Trail

104

31   College Avenue

The descent through Devil's Hole makes this one of the most dramatic spots in the Niagara Falls Gorge.

Proceed down this trail to see the famous whirlpool and rapids.) Head up the stairs to the rim.

1.7 Reach the Rim Trail. Turn left and walk along the rim to the Devil's Hole trailhead.

2.5 Arrive back at the pedestrian bridge to the parking area.

38 Old Fort Niagara State Historic Site / Beach Trail

This historic site predates the French and Indian Wars. You can walk along lookout points that French soldiers occupied as far back as the 1600s.

Start: Parking area at Old Fort Niagara in Fort Niagara State Park
Distance: 1.1-mile loop
Hiking time: About 45 minutes
Elevation gain: 63 feet
High point: 281 feet
Difficulty: Easy
Best season: Summer and fall
Traffic: Hikers only

Fees and permits: Park entrance fee Memorial Day through Labor Day; will be subtracted from your ticket to tour the fort
Maps: Fort Niagara State Park brochure, available at the park entrance
Trail contacts: Fort Niagara State Park, NY 18F, Youngstown 14174; (716) 745-7273; nysparks.com/historic-sites/31/details.aspx

Finding the trailhead: From I-190 North, take exit 25B toward NY 104 (Robert Moses Parkway). Merge onto Upper Mountain Road, and keep left at the fork on NY 104 / Robert Moses Parkway. Merge onto the parkway and drive 8 miles to the exit for NY 18F / Fort Niagara. Follow the signs to Fort Niagara as you take a slight right onto Scott Avenue. The park will be on your right. Park in the large parking area near the interpretive signs and the snack bar. The hike begins by crossing picnic area #3. GPS: N43 15.875' / W79 03.366'

The Hike

We've made the assumption that while you are at Fort Niagara State Park, you will take advantage of the opportunity to tour the 300-year-old Old Fort Niagara. Stop at the visitor center and see the informational movie about the fort, visit the history museum, and then walk through two centuries of military installations, from the 1726 French castle to the land defenses and casemate gallery, both circa 1872. Your visit will give context to the strategic position the rest of this park once held in the battles between French, British, and American troops stationed here on this lookout point between the United States and Canada.

Once you've visited the fort, this hike begins from the other major parking area in the state park—not the one with the lighthouse; the one with modern conveniences including a snack bar. You may want to walk over to the larger parking area, but keep in mind that the fort parking lot fills up on a busy day, so as a courtesy to others, make the move to the state park lot.

From the parking area, proceed east along the bluff to the trailhead. This trail leads along the lakeshore to provide spectacular views of Lake Ontario as it meets the Niagara River. This is one of the closest points to Canada on the south shore of the lake, so you can actually see Toronto fairly well on a clear day. Look for the lofty CN

Historical Background

Here stands Old Fort Niagara, the longest continually occupied military site in the United States and the oldest building on the Great Lakes. Fort Niagara guarded the mouth of the Niagara River, the strategically critical point of access to the Great Lakes and the continent beyond, making it an attractive and hotly contested position for three different nations until the end of the Revolutionary War.

Before the fort's earliest construction, the Iroquois Confederacy controlled the mouth of the Niagara River, as the French discovered when they penetrated the interior of the New World and came down the St. Lawrence River from Canada. The French clashed repeatedly with the Iroquois for decades throughout the seventeenth century, until explorer René-Robert Cavelier, Sieur de La Salle, arrived in 1679 and made a tenuous truce with the native peoples. He managed to get the Iroquois to grant him permission to use the river, establishing the French in a small post on this promontory while he prepared to sail upriver. La Salle's men built a stockade and called it Fort Conti, but shortly after the explorers sailed off for parts west, the stockade burned down. The remaining Frenchmen walked away from the outpost with no plans to return.

Nonetheless, French forces returned to the point in the fall of 1687, as an army led by the Marquis de Denonville wreaked havoc throughout the Seneca towns in western New York. Despite repeated attacks, however, Denonville could not gain a foothold in the region, and he essentially trapped himself and his men on this promontory over the winter of 1687, with inadequate supplies against the legendary Niagara winter. Cut off from access to supply routes by Seneca warriors determined to freeze out the French, Denonville's men perished from hunger and cold. When spring arrived, only a dozen men remained. The French sent reinforcements, but in the fall of 1688, they too abandoned the post.

The fort we see here today was built in 1726 under the guise of a trading post, a structure the Iroquois Confederacy agreed to allow—but without the Seneca at the table. When the final construction and the arrival of armed soldiers made it clear that this was more than a center of trade, the Seneca objected—and so did the British.

This end-run by the French resulted in their taking control of the portage around Niagara Falls, a position the British found untenably inconvenient. One conflict after another rocked the relationship between British and French colonists until the British finally besieged the fort during the French and Indian War, forcing the French to surrender on July 25, 1759.

The British held the fort until nearly thirteen years after they lost the Revolutionary War, as disputes over borders and trade relations lingered even though the battles had ended. The US Army took over the fort on August 10, 1796, and kept it until December 19, 1813, the day the British staged a surprise attack in the midst of the War of 1812 and took back this strategic post.

Just outside Lewiston on the Niagara River, a blue history sign marks the spot where the British Regulars came ashore on the night of December 18, 1813, and began their march north to capture Fort Niagara. Stinging from an American assault on the British-held town of Newark on December 10, the Regulars began a retaliatory strike that took the American forces entirely by surprise on the night of December 19, while Fort Niagara's commander, Nathanial Leonard, was visiting family in Lewiston. In a cascade failure of the fort's defenses, the picket soldiers left to guard the fort had succumbed to the cold and gone inside. The British disarmed the Youngstown pickets easily and without bloodshed, gained entrance to the fort itself when the gates opened to admit an American, and found just about the fort's entire complement fast asleep. By sunrise, Fort Niagara was a British outpost. The Regulars used the fort as a base of operations as they advanced to destroy Youngstown, Lewiston, Manchester, Fort Schlosser, Black Rock, and Buffalo.

The Regulars were forced to give up the fort in 1815 under the Treaty of Ghent, which ended the War of 1812. Once secured by the Americans again, the fort remained an active military post until it became part of Fort Niagara State Park in the 1960s. Today the restored fort serves as the keeper and interpreter of the military history that shaped this entire region.

Be sure to see Old Fort Niagara while you visit the park.

Tower, the easiest identifying landmark to spot from here. (A cold winter day can be the best time to achieve this view.)

You have the option of hiking along the lakeshore and then turning around and coming back that way, or of following the park boundary to the access road and walking back along it to complete a loop. We hiked here in mid-May and found the walk back along the road to be surprisingly pleasant, with many wildflowers growing along the verge and a remarkable number of bird species feeding in the trees. Try out this hike during spring or fall migration at this key stopover point and you may find yourself delighted by the number of passerines—warblers, vireos, and other migrants—that allow you good, close looks as they rest and feed before continuing their journey north or south.

Miles and Directions

0.0 Start from the parking area and walk east along the mowed area to the trailhead.

0.2 Reach the trailhead. A nicely maintained dirt path leads into the woods.

0.3 Turn left for the scenic overlook. From this point on the Lake Ontario coastline, on a clear day you can see Toronto, Ontario. The trail continues to your right. There's another scenic overlook in about 100 feet. Watch your step at both of these—there are no guardrails or fences, and the bluffs may be eroded underneath you. If you look down, you'll see trees growing on the beach that used to stand right about where you are now.

New York's North Coast features rugged cliffs and rocky bluffs.

Old Fort Niagara State Historic Site/Beach Trail

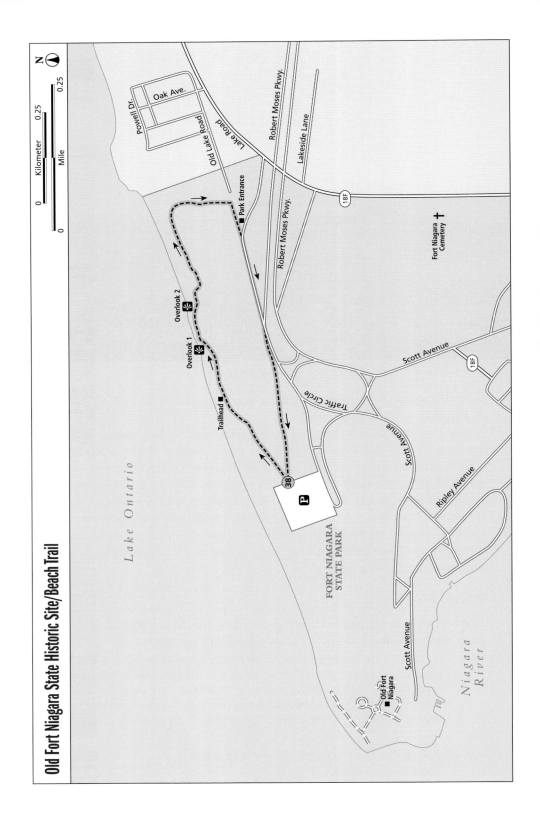

0.5 To the left, another scenic view is visible, though it may be obscured by tall wildflowers in summer. Turn right. You can see a mansion through the trees here; it's a private residence, so let it be. A gate to the mansion becomes visible to your left. Turn right to stay on the trail.

0.6 Emerge at the park entrance road. From here you can return the way you came (and enjoy the views again) or follow the road straight ahead, walking on the mowed grass to complete the loop. There are lots of wildflowers and a nice variety of woodpeckers along this verge, so it's worth walking the park road back to your vehicle.

1.1 Arrive back at the parking area.

39 Letchworth State Park: Lower, Upper, and Middle Falls Area

Explore "The Grand Canyon of the East" for a touch of early American history and some of the best scenic waterfall views in upstate New York.

Start: Lower Falls parking area at the Castile end of the park
Distance: 4.2 miles
Hiking time: About 2 hours
Elevation gain: 413 feet
High point: 1,031 feet
Difficulty: Moderate (many steps)
Best season: Spring and fall
Traffic: Hikers only

Fees and permits: Fee per car on weekends Memorial Day through Labor Day
Maps: Park maps available online at nysparks.com/parks/79/maps.aspx
Trail contact: Letchworth State Park, 1 Letchworth State Park, Castile 14427; (585) 493-3600; nysparks.com/parks/79
Special considerations: Some roads in the park are closed Dec 1 to Apr 1.

Finding the trailhead: From Rochester take I-390 South to exit 7 for Mount Morris / Letchworth Park. Turn left onto NY 408 South. Follow NY 408 for 2 miles to the park entrance. Enter the park and drive 16 miles on the park road to the falls area. Pass the Lower Falls/Restaurant turnoff and continue to the right to reach the Lower Falls parking area. GPS: N42 35.371' / W78 00.651'

The Hike

For thousands of years after the last ice age, the Genesee River—a waterway whose course altered significantly when glacial activity relocated it—wore a deep crevasse into the earth here at the south end of its length. The river continues north to Rochester, until it finally empties into Lake Ontario, but this state-protected area contains its most dramatic canyon, accented by three powerful waterfalls in the space of 2 miles.

Geologists believe that these falls formed sequentially as the glaciers melted, retaining the meltwater in temporary lakes until erosion took the flow over the side. Sandstone holds the falls in place, resisting the river's erosive power, while layers of shale and sandstone form the supporting natural structure. The falls area provides many viewpoints from which you can study the walls of the 550-foot-deep gorge.

You can walk the entire length of the falls area in less than an hour. Many sets of stone stairs help you reach the falls overlook platforms with relative ease; don't be shy about pausing on a landing or halfway up a stairway to catch your breath. During the fall foliage season, this area can be congested with bumper-to-bumper traffic, so walking between the falls may provide the most comfortable and satisfying way to see them.

In addition to the three waterfalls, this end of Letchworth State Park offers the Glen Iris Inn, a historic hotel and restaurant; concessions in season, picnic areas, a gift shop, and modern restrooms.

Historical Background

Beyond the geological story of Letchworth State Park lie two decidedly different human stories, histories of individuals whose lives played important roles in this segment of the Genesee Valley. The first is Mary Jemison, the daughter of Scotch-Irish immigrants who arrived in America in 1743. During the French and Indian War, Mary, her parents, and three of her siblings were captured by raiding French and Shawnee soldiers in 1758. As the party headed west, the Shawnee warriors killed and scalped the members of the Jemison family—except for Mary, whom they sold to a band of Seneca from the territory that later became Ohio. Mary grew up among the Seneca, who named her Dehgewanus, or "Two Falling Voices," and she eventually moved to the Letchworth area with her Seneca husband, Shenijee, who did not survive the 700-mile journey.

Living among the Seneca people near the Genesee River, Dehgewanus remarried and raised seven children until the Revolutionary War, when her tribe sided with the British—making them a prime target for the Continental Army. Dehgewanus fled with her children, finding shelter and relative safety in an abandoned Seneca village to the south. Here she lived for more than five decades. As the area became more populated with white settlers after the war, Dehgewanus became famous for her generosity to those in need, as well as for her colorful past. The neighbors called her "The Old White Woman of the Genesee," and a biography, *A Narrative of the Life of Mrs. Mary Jemison*, written in 1823 by James E. Seaver, became a popular seller. You can pick up a copy in the park's gift shop. Or visit the recently renovated and expanded William Pryor Letchworth Museum, where you can learn more about the local Native Americans and their place in New York history.

Who was William Pryor Letchworth? A Buffalo businessman looking for a way to escape the pressures of enterprise, Letchworth came to the Genesee Valley in

(Continued)

the late 1850s when he heard about property owned by Michael Smith and Theodore Olcott, who bought their acreage in the 1830s because they believed the area soon would become popular with tourists. After many years of renting out the building on the property to tenants, however, Smith found himself struggling to make ends meet. In 1859 he sold his land and buildings—and their accompanying debt—to Letchworth for $1, while Olcott got $7,000 from Letchworth to pay off Smith's mortgage. The new owner immediately began plans for Glen Iris, the home he would build by extending and modernizing the old Cataract House, as well as renovations of the barns and outbuildings and landscaping of the extensive grounds around the house. So thoroughly did Letchworth re-create the residential areas here, they began to attract tourists, just as Smith and Olcott had predicted a generation earlier. Letchworth welcomed visitors through the gates and onto the grounds, where they could admire his gardens and the nearby Council Grounds as well as the magnificent waterfalls at his front door. In 1907, as he entered his waning years, Letchworth gave his Glen Iris Estate, including 1,000 acres of open land, to the State of New York for creation of a park. He lived out his last days here at Glen Iris, until his death on December 1, 1910.

Miles and Directions

0.0 Start from the Lower Falls parking area. Walk past the Footbridge Nature Shoppe and the picnic area and pavilion to the Lower Falls Trail (you'll see a brown-and-yellow sign).

0.2 You have two options: Walk down 127 stairs to the best viewpoint, or go to your right for the easy viewpoint in about 1,000 feet. If you take the stairs, continue straight at the bottom of the staircase on the flat trail, with the gorge to your left.

0.3 Reach the Lower Falls Overlook. The trail curves out here, giving you a viewpoint that's clear of the trees. Continue on the trail to Table Rock.

0.4 Come to Table Rock. There's a wide viewing area here with an additional lower platform and a bridge across the river. Go down forty-eight steps for an amazing view of the falls. Take the bridge over the river just for the experience; there's no view of the waterfall on the other side. When you're ready, either return to your car the way you came (0.4 mile back) and drive to the next parking area, or continue to walk down the trail between the falls, on the path along the stone wall.

1.8 Walk down ten steps to the overlook point at the top of Middle Falls. This is the most spectacular of the three waterfalls, and there's plenty of room on the stone platform for good views. Continue along the stone wall to additional overlook points in front of the falls. Check the walls of the gorge for a little bridal veil falls in a particularly green spot (to your left as you look at Middle Falls).

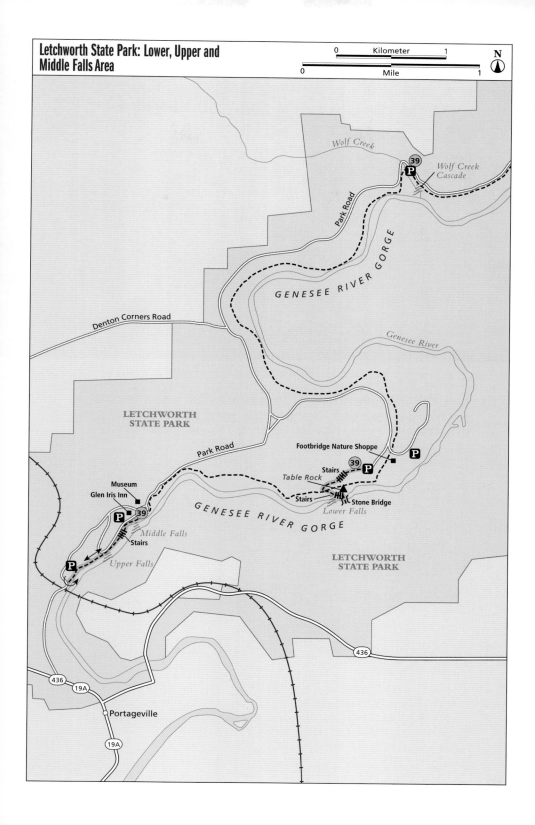

Wolf Creek

39

Wolf Creek Cascade

Park Road

GENESEE RIVER GORGE

Genesee River

Denton Corners Road

LETCHWORTH STATE PARK

Park Road

Footbridge Nature Shoppe

P

Stairs

39

P

Museum

Table Rock

Glen Iris Inn

39

Stairs

Stone Bridge

P

Lower Falls

Middle Falls

GENESEE RIVER GORGE

Stairs

LETCHWORTH STATE PARK

P

Upper Falls

436

436

19A

Portageville

19A

Few places in New York can surpass the visual splendor of Letchworth State Park.

2.1 Arrive at the first overlook for Upper Falls. Continue on the path for more views of Upper Falls. When you're ready, return from Upper Falls on the trail along the stone wall at the edge of the gorge, and head back down to the Lower Falls parking area.

4.2 Arrive back at the parking area.

40 Newtown Battlefield State Park

A peaceful amble through the site of one of New York's most volatile and important Revolutionary War battles.

Start: Parking area at Newtown Battlefield State Park

Distance: 0.8-mile loop

Hiking time: About 30 minutes

Elevation gain: 149 feet

High point: 1,465 feet

Difficulty: Easy

Best season: Spring through fall

Traffic: Hikers, trail runners

Fees and permits: Vehicle use fee at entrance in peak seasons

Maps: Park map available online at nysparks.com/parks/attachments/NewtownBattlefield ParkMap.pdf

Trail contacts: Newtown Battlefield State Park, 2346 CR 60, Elmira 14901; (607) 732-6067; nysparks.com/parks/107

Finding the trailhead: From I-86 (NY 17) take exit 56 for NY 352 toward Elmira. At the end of the exit ramp, turn left onto NY 352 East (East Water Street). Bear right onto Jerusalem Hill Road, and then turn right onto Brant Road. Continue 1.8 miles as Brant becomes Oneida Road. The park entrance is on the right in about 1.5 miles at the intersection with Newtown Reservation Road. The street address is 2346 CR 60, Elmira. GPS: N42 02.736' / W76 44.042'

The Hike

This fairly short hike follows a ridgeline named for the Sullivan Campaign, a lesser-known (at least, outside of New York) but critical segment of the United States' defense against British troops during the Revolutionary War. Iroquois Confederacy soldiers fighting on the side of the English Crown met their match here at Newtown as they joined with Loyalist rangers and Redcoats to take on the Continental Army. The battle raged up and down Sullivan's Hill, terrain covered with pine and shrub oak and sloping more than 600 feet down from the crest of the rise. You may be pleased to know that this hike does not range very far up and down the hill; instead it follows just below the top of the hill and circles back on the edge of the central battleground.

The hike begins at the granite monument on the hilltop. This monument, placed here by the Civilian Conservation Corps in the 1930s, replaces the original stone monument erected in 1879 on the battle's centennial. After visiting the monument, continue to the observation deck to the east for one of the finest views you'll find anywhere of the Chemung Valley, a highlight of New York's Southern Tier. Bear left off the platform and follow the paved path to the Sullivan's March Trailhead.

The narrow, slanting path through the woods feels fairly rugged because of its hillside angle and covering of woodland detritus, and it dips and rises along its 0.5-mile length until its junction with the Newtown Pike Trail. Trail markings only occur at

Historical Background

At the beginning of the Revolutionary War, the Six Nations of the Iroquois Confederacy originally planned to stay out of what they considered to be a private conflict between the British and the new Americans. One Iroquois chief, however—a Mohawk named Joseph Brant—chose to side with the British, opposing the American colonists who had taken control of so much of the land originally held by the Iroquois peoples. He warned other tribes that if they stayed out of the war and the Americans won, they would lose more land to the new country, while the British, grateful for the Iroquois support, would make a fair deal with the Six Nations at the end of the war. Eventually he convinced the Mohawk, Cayuga, Onondaga, and Seneca to fight with the British. When it became clear that neutrality was not an option, the Oneida and the Tuscarora sided with the Americans.

Under Brant's leadership as a captain in the British army, the four Iroquois nations carried out a series of bloody raids on American farmers and farming communities throughout New York State, most notably in Cobleskill, Wyoming Valley, and Cherry Valley. They destroyed harvested food and crops to keep these supplies from reaching Gen. George Washington's army, and many farmers and their families died defending their homes during these surprise attacks. British Loyalists assisted in these raids as well, but the Americans knew that the way to put a stop to these marauders led through the Indian villages throughout southern and western New York.

Washington and the Continental Congress designated an army of 4,000 soldiers to punish the Iroquois for their loyalty to the British, naming Maj. Gen. John Sullivan and Brig. Gen. James Clinton to lead the retaliatory strikes. The Sullivan-Clinton Campaign set out across the states of Pennsylvania (led by Sullivan) and New York (commanded by Clinton) as aggressively as had their Iroquois adversaries, carrying

(Continued)

A monument at the top of the park commemorates the battle at Newtown.

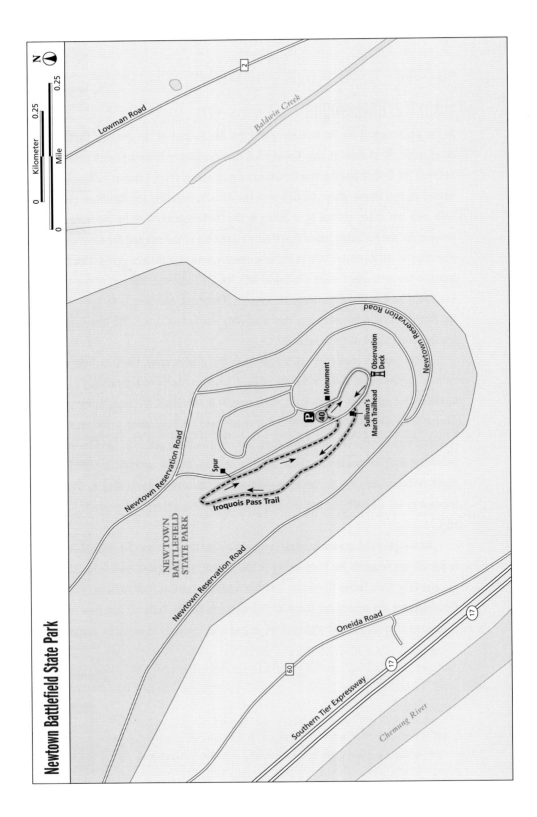

Newtown Battlefield State Park

out a "scorched earth" campaign in which they burned at least forty villages, torched orchards and cornfields, and killed any and all Iroquois they found—including civilian villagers. Many fled ahead of the oncoming military force, hiding in the forests and dying by the hundreds of starvation and exposure.

The only direct confrontation between Sullivan and Clinton's men and the British and Iroquois army took place here at Newtown on August 29, 1779, where the British and Indian troops had built earthworks to disguise their strategic position partway up the hill. Sullivan's forces spotted the earthworks and began an attack meant to draw out the hidden Loyalists while taking them by surprise—not an easy feat on short notice, but one the Continental forces executed more than effectively, even thwarting counterattacks by Captain Brant and his combined British and Iroquois forces. At the end of the day, casualties on the Continental side numbered fewer than 100, while the British and Iroquois forces lost more than 1,000 men.

After the battle, Sullivan's army continued its sweep through southern New York, destroying three more Iroquois towns near Newtown before turning north and marching for another three weeks through the Finger Lakes region. When the war ended in 1781, the Iroquois nations had been all but destroyed. Only about 8,000 Iroquois remained in New York State—a tiny fraction of the Six Nations Confederacy—and they never recovered from their terrible losses.

intersections, so you'll need to use your best judgment as to whether you are still on the right route. Once you join the Newtown Pike, however, the trail becomes wider and flatter. The route described here circles back to the parking area on Newtown Pike, but you have the option of lengthening your hike by continuing west, crossing the park on this very pleasant trail.

Miles and Directions

0.0 Start from the parking area and proceed to the monument at the top of the hill. Follow the paved path to the observation deck.

0.1 When you are ready to proceed, bear left off the platform and follow the paved path to the Sullivan's March Trailhead. Head northwest on the trail.

0.4 The Iroquois Pass Trail goes right. Continue straight.

0.5 At the junction with Newtown Pike, turn right to complete the loop.

0.6 At the junction with a spur that leads back to the paved loop, continue straight.

0.8 Emerge at the Newtown Pike Trailhead, and head back to your vehicle.

Appendix: Clubs and Trail Groups

Adirondack Mountain Club: Albany Chapter, PO Box 2116, ESP Sta., Albany 12220; (518) 899-2725; adk-albany.org. Genesee Valley Chapter, PO Box 18558, Rochester 14618; (585) 987-1717; gvc-adk.org. Niagara Frontier Chapter; adk-nfc .org. Onondaga Chapter; adk-on.org. The club in each region offers a variety of hikes and programs to share the joy and knowledge of outdoor recreation.

Appalachian Mountain Club: Mohawk-Hudson Chapter; amcmohawkhudson .org. Formed to promote the protection and wise use of the Northeast's mountains, rivers, and trails, the club offers many outings and recreational opportunities through-out the year.

Audubon Society of the Capital Region: PO Box 11654, Albany 12211; www .capitalregionaudubon.org. The Capital chapter of the Audubon Society conserves and protects birds and wildlife habitat through advocacy and education. It offers field trips, sanctuary management, and environmental education.

Buffalo Audubon Society: 1610 Welch Rd., North Java 14113; (800) 377-1520; buffaloaudubon.com. With several preserves of its own, Buffalo Audubon promotes appreciation and enjoyment of the natural world. Look for events and hikes on its website.

Buffalo Niagara Riverkeeper: 617 Main St., Suite M108, Buffalo 14203; (716) 852-7483; bnriverkeeper.org. This organization improves public waterfront access, restores watershed ecology, and conserves the river heritage.

Burroughs Audubon Nature Club: PO Box 26814, Rochester 14626; bancny .org. This organization of nature lovers owns its own preserve near the Auburn Trail Railroad Mills section.

Catskill Mountain Club: PO Box 558, Pine Hill 12465. Outdoor recreational activities, volunteer stewardship of public resources, and environmental advocacy.

Chautauqua Rails to Trails: NY 394 in the Train Depot, PO Box 151, Mayville 14757; (716) 269-3666;.chaurtt.org. This organization is dedicated to the preserva-tion of abandoned rail corridors as trails for recreational use.

Foothills Trail Club: foothillstrailclub.org. Creators of the 177-mile Conservation Trail, this group's membership is dedicated to building and maintaining trails, aid-ing in the conservation of wild lands and wildlife, and promoting good fellowship through hikes and nature.

Genesee Valley Hiking Club: (585) 359-0902; gvhchikes.org. Members lead many hikes—often three in a week—from the Rochester area to the Finger Lakes Trail in the Southern Tier.

Interstate Hiking Club: 33 Morris Ave., PO Box 52, Mt. Tabor, NJ 07878; interstatehikingclub.org. This club organizes hiking, canoeing, biking, snowshoeing, and maintenance trips Friday through Sunday in northern New Jersey and southern New York.

Long Path North Hiking Club: Schoharie-conservation.org/memberclubs/lpn/index.html. Formed as an offshoot of the New York/New Jersey Trail Conference, this organization constructs and maintains the Long Path and offers hikes on the trail in every season.

New York–New Jersey Trail Conference: 156 Ramapo Valley Rd., Mahwah, NJ 07430; (201) 512-9348; nynjtc.org. The leading authority on trails in the New York–New Jersey metropolitan region, the conference works in partnership with parks to create and protect a network of more than 1,700 miles of trails.

Onondaga Audubon Society: PO Box 620, Syracuse 13201; onondagaaudubon.org. Onondaga Audubon promotes a greater appreciation of wildlife, land, water, and other natural resources through field trips, sanctuary management, and environmental education.

Rip Van Winkle Hikers: 18 John St., Saugerties 12477; (845) 246-8074; newyorkheritage.com/rvw. This club hosts year-round hikes in the Catskills and Mid-Hudson for people of every skill level.

Sierra Club, Mid-Hudson Group: PO Box 1012, Poughkeepsie 12602; newyork.sierraclub.org/midhudson. The club offers weekly hiking or canoe trips for people of all skill levels, as well as activities for national and local conservation.

Syracuse Area Outdoor Adventure Club: meetup.com/adventurers-103. For people who want to get outside, have fun, and meet others with similar interests, the group holds regularly scheduled hikes and seasonal adventures.

Syracuse University Outing Club: suoc.syr.edu. Students of Syracuse University and the SUNY College of Environmental Science and Forestry join to promote the enjoyment of the national environment with many trips and outings.

Taconic Hiking Club: 29 Campagna Dr., Albany 12205; taconichikingclub.blogspot.com. For people interested in nature study, hiking, backpacking, camping, cycling, canoeing, kayaking, snowshoeing, cross-country skiing, and more.

Victor Hiking Trails, Inc.: (585) 234-8226; victorhikingtrails.org. Stewards of the Auburn Trail, sections of the Lehigh Valley Trail, and others, this grassroots organization promotes individual responsibility for protecting the environment.

Westchester Trails Association: westhike.org. Hikes and outdoor events are scheduled on Saturday and Sunday throughout the year.

Hike Index

About the Author and Photographer

Wife-and-husband team **Randi and Nic Minetor** have collaborated on twenty books about hiking, exploring historic cities, America's national parks, and birds and nature. Their popular books on outdoor activities in New York State include five books in FalconGuides' Best Easy Day Hikes series on Rochester, Buffalo, Syracuse, Albany, and the Hudson River Valley, as well as the popular *Hiking Waterfalls in New York* and *Scenic Routes and Byways New York*. They also worked together on eight Quick Reference Guides to the native birds, trees, and wildflowers of New York State, New York City, and Long Island, and of the Mid-Atlantic states. Avid birders and seasoned road-trippers, the Minetors also collaborated on the best-selling *Backyard Birding: A Guide to Attracting and Identifying Birds* (Lyons Press) and *New England Bird Lover's Garden* (Globe Pequot).

When not in the car or on the trail, Randi is a freelance writer for corporations, executives, and nonprofit organizations; Nic is the resident lighting designer for several theatre and opera companies in upstate New York and for the PBS series *Second Opinion*. The Minetors live in Rochester, New York.

Nic and Randi Minetor

American Hiking Society

Because you **hike.**
We're with you every step of the way

As a national voice for hikers, **American Hiking Society** works every day:

- Building and maintaining hiking trails
- Educating and supporting hikers by providing information and resources
- Supporting hiking and trail organizations nationwide
- Speaking for hikers in the halls of Congress and with federal land managers

Whether you're a casual hiker or a seasoned backpacker, become a member of American Hiking Society and join the national hiking community! You'll enjoy great member benefits and help preserve the nation's hiking trails, so tomorrow's hike is even better than today's. We invite you to join us now!

American Hiking Society